eating in

Dearest Mary —
Eating in at "Chez Loxton"
is always the best —
there won't be anything better —
here that you don't do better —
but it comes with
love anyway
Natalie x

eating in

the ultimate comfort food for entertaining at home

Alison Price and Nanette Newman

Kyle Cathie Ltd

acknowledgements

Creating a book involves not just the authors: I'd like to thank Dave Withers for testing all the recipes apart from the desserts, which fell into the very creative hands of Paul North and Anthony Saunders; Dave and Petri Poysti for recreating the recipes for the camera; Bill and Rob for running around and collecting the bits and pieces and Sarah White for reading the first draft and adding great comments in the columns such as, 'Yummy!', and, 'I can't wait to try this!'. Also thanks to James Murphy for his fantastic photographs and his team for making the photo shoots a really fun time, Antonia Gaunt for her creative styling and Helen Woodhall our editor for her support, encouragement, patience, sense of humour, and for allowing us to bring our ideas to create *Eating In*. Nanette, working with you has been a fun time and very creative, and thanks are due to Bryan for being our taster and guinea pig, as well as to friends for the ideas on what they like to cook at home. *Alison*

I join Alison in saying an enormous thank you to the creative team who worked on this book, and a big thank you from me to Alison herself. *Nanette*

First published in Great Britain 2005 by
Kyle Cathie Limited
122 Arlington Road
London NW1 7HP
general.enquiries@kyle-cathie.com
www.kylecathie.com

ISBN 1 85626 568 4

Text © Alison Price and Nanette Newman
Photography © James Murphy
Book design © Kyle Cathie Limited

Editor: Helen Woodhall
Editorial Assistant: Sophie Allen
Designer: www.pinkstripedesign.com
Photographer: James Murphy
Styling: Antonia Gaunt
Copyeditor: Anne Newman
Production: Sha Huxtable

A Cataloguing in Publication record for
this title is available from the British Library.

Colour reproduction by Sang Choy, Singapore
Printed and bound in Singapore by KHL Printing Co.

This book is dedicated to the memory of Patrick White who so much enjoyed cooking and sharing wonderful food and great wines with his family and friends

Alison

contents

introduction

When two friends decide to write a cookbook, it's inevitable that the pre-amble to putting pen to paper takes up a lot of time. Well, at least it did with us because we enjoyed it so much.

We spent many pleasurable hours chatting about the meals we thought were wonderful, the friend who's made the 'to-die-for' cake, the way they cooked the fish in the restaurant in that tiny Italian village, the Sunday lunch with lots of children when someone whipped up a mouth-watering pudding in minutes, and there was even one afternoon when we sat in the garden drinking chilled white wine talking about the best potato dish we'd ever eaten (on page 117 by the way).

It made us realise that the pleasure of food is invariably linked to how much you enjoyed the occasion and the people you were with.

We both decided that although we loved eating out, we really loved eating in. We also agreed that we adored the type of food that comes under the very large umbrella of comfort food – meals you have in relaxed, no-fuss surroundings with family and friends, sometimes in celebration but mostly a putting-together of food, wine and company for no better reason than you want to be together and share a meal.

Our conversations about the book were always being side-tracked by memories of places and people as much as by the food itself.

When we had talked a lot, sorted out recipe notes, argued about favourite methods, discussed the type of cookery books we didn't like as well as those we did, we came to the conclusion that our book was going to be for people like us, people who love to cook and who get turned on by reading about cooking but who don't want to go demented in the kitchen trying to create something hellishly complicated that is better suited to a restaurant. We like short cuts, we like new ideas and we also love the old favourites that have stood the test of time. And, of course, we agree (and so do you) that the basic products have to be the freshest and best available in order to produce superb homemade food.

Finally, we began putting down our favourite recipes gathered from different places, countries and friends. We tried to include all the things we like to cook and love to eat. So, here it is. We hope you'll enjoy the result and that, when you want to get a few new ideas, you'll look through our book and find just what you want when you're 'eating-in'.

Lazy Sunday Breakfast

To many of us, breakfast is a quick cup of coffee and a piece of toast. Or, if you have children, a dippy egg with soldiers made with one eye on the clock knowing you're going to be late for the school run. But there are a few occasions when you have time for a bit of a lie-in, a late breakfast or brunch with the Sunday papers. When this blissful event occurs you might as well make the most of it, and have a breakfast that is special. These recipes are to be shared with someone on days when work is the last thing you have to think about.

Morning sunrise

600ml (1 pint) fresh orange juice
600ml (1 pint) fresh pineapple juice
1 ripe banana
Ice cubes
Splash of grenadine (optional)
Slices of orange or pineapple, to garnish

Serves 4

Place the orange juice, pineapple juice and banana into a blender and blend on a high speed until smooth. Fill glasses with ice, pour over the juice, top with a splash of grenadine if you wish, garnish with the fruit slices and serve.

Berry smoothie

90g (3oz) strawberries, hulled
60g (2½oz) blackberries
60g (2½oz) raspberries
4 tablespoons low-fat Greek yogurt
Ice cubes
Sugar, to taste

Serves 2

Place all the ingredients in a blender with about 8 ice cubes and blend until smooth. Taste, add sugar if you need it, and serve.

Apple, lime and ginger refresher

1 litre (2 pints) sharp-tasting organic apple juice
Juice of 4 limes
1 tablespoon grated root ginger
Lime slices and slices of root ginger, to garnish

Serves 4

Mix all the ingredients in a large jug and place in the fridge. Serve cold, garnished with slices of lime and ginger.

Rhubarb smoothie

300ml (½ pint) poached rhubarb
350g (12oz) low-fat Greek yogurt
2 teaspoons grated root ginger
Ice cubes
Sugar, to taste

Serves 2

Place all the ingredients in a blender with about 6 ice cubes and blend until smooth. Taste, add sugar if needed, and serve.

For really fresh fruit juices, invest in a juicer, then you're able to make homemade drinks at any time. Otherwise, buy good quality fresh fruit juice.

Fat and fluffy French toast

This is a variation on the usual French toast, but made with panettone, which is a great standby in your store cupboard. You can gild the lily with a drizzle of maple syrup or honey if you wish.

½ teaspoon vanilla extract
2 large free-range eggs, beaten
Pinch of salt
125ml (4fl oz) full-fat milk
1 teaspoon mixed spice
4 slices panettone
110g (4oz) granola
60g (2½oz) unsalted butter

Serves 2

In a mixing bowl whisk together the vanilla, eggs, salt, milk and spice. Dip the panettone slices into the mixture, then coat them with the granola. Heat the butter in a heavy non-stick frying pan and fry the panettone on each side until golden brown and crispy. Serve immediately on warm plates.

> If you don't have panettone, try raisin bread instead.

Baked eggs with pitta bread soldiers

For total luxury you could serve the baked eggs turned out onto plates and topped with a spoonful of caviar. The setting for this should be pure Noël Coward.

60g (2½oz) unsalted butter, at room
    temperature, plus extra for greasing
Small handful of chives, snipped
4 large free-range eggs, at room
    temperature
Sea salt and ground white pepper
2 tablespoons double cream
8 mini pitta breads

Serves 4

Preheat the oven to 200°C/400°F/gas mark 6 and preheat the grill. Butter 4 egg cocotte dishes or small ramekins. Cream the butter and chives together.

Crack an egg into each cocotte and season. Pour the cream over the eggs. Place the dishes in a roasting tin, pour 2.5cm (1in) boiling water into the tin and place in the oven for 8 minutes or until the egg whites are set but the yolks are still runny.

Meanwhile, toast the pitta breads under the grill. Remove, spread with the chive butter, cut into strips and keep warm. Remove the eggs from the oven, dry the outsides of the dishes and place on plates. Serve immediately with the pitta bread soldiers.

Melon and mint

There are no set rules for this. Just buy really good melons in season and cube, slice or ball them – whatever takes your fancy – place them in a bowl, turn with some finely shredded mint leaves and serve ice-cold.

Sophia's special eggs benedict

My friend Sophia loves Eggs Benedict and this is her version. We spent time perfecting the cheat's hollandaise; she also likes to top the Parma ham with a few spears of asparagus. Eggs Benedict is another of those dishes that has gone out of fashion – it's definitely worth a comeback. *Alison*

2 large free-range eggs
1 English breakfast muffin, cut in half
4 slices Parma ham

FOR THE CHEAT'S HOLLANDAISE SAUCE
3 large free-range egg yolks
4 teaspoons freshly squeezed
  lemon juice
150g (5oz) unsalted butter
Sea salt and ground white pepper

Serves 2

Fill a saucepan with water, bring to the boil and simmer. Preheat the grill.

To make the cheat's hollandaise, blend the egg yolks and lemon juice in a blender or food processor. Meanwhile, melt the butter until foaming and bubbling, pour into a jug and slowly add to the egg mixture, keeping the blender running. Remove, season and keep warm. The sauce should resemble lightly whipped double cream.

Crack the eggs into separate cups, being careful not to break the yolks. Drop the eggs carefully into the water and poach until the whites are set. While the eggs are poaching, toast the muffin halves and grill the Parma ham until crisp. Using a slotted spoon, carefully remove the eggs from the water on to a plate.

To serve, place 2 slices of Parma ham on each muffin half, top with a poached egg and spoon over the hollandaise.

If the sauce begins to curdle, add 3 teaspoons of hot water, with the blender still running, and mix until smooth again.

The red omelette

This is a hearty omelette – and if you have it for breakfast it will set you up for the day.

1 red pepper, roasted, skinned,
  deseeded and chopped
2 plum tomatoes, peeled, deseeded
  and chopped
60g (2½oz) mature Cheddar cheese,
  grated
1 tablespoon sunflower oil
60g (2½oz) spicy chorizo, sliced
½ red onion, finely chopped
25g (1oz) unsalted butter
4 large free-range eggs
2 tablespoons cold water
Sea salt and ground paprika

Serves 2

Place the red pepper, tomatoes and cheese in a bowl and mix well. Leave to one side.

Heat a medium, heavy, non-stick frying pan and add the oil. When it is hot, add the chorizo and onion and sauté until the onion is soft. Remove, drain on kitchen paper and set aside. Pour the oil from cooking the chorizo into a jug.

Clean the pan, return to the heat and add the reserved oil and the butter. In a bowl, whisk the eggs together with the water and season with salt and a little paprika. Working fast, pour half the egg mixture into the hot pan, reduce the heat to medium and simultaneously whisk the eggs and shake the pan vigorously back and forth over the heat for less than a minute. You want to keep the eggs moving, incorporating the runny with the more-cooked parts. Make sure the mixture covers the surface of the pan.

Scatter over half the pepper mixture, chorizo and onion. Shake the pan, fold the omelette in half using a rubber spatula and gently press together. Leave for about 1 minute to allow the cheese to melt, remove from the heat and slide on to a warm plate. Repeat the process for the second omelette.

Skinned red peppers can be bought ready-made in jars.

Breakfast in a tomato

This is a great combination of flavours. Make sure you use really large, ripe tomatoes.

4 large tomatoes
4 rashers smoked streaky bacon
60g (2½oz) black pudding (if you do not wish to use black pudding, increase the amount of bacon to 8 rashers)
25g (1oz) unsalted butter
60g (2½oz) button mushrooms, finely sliced
Sea salt and ground black pepper
4 small free-range eggs, at room temperature
Hot buttered toast, to serve

Serves 2

Preheat the oven to 190°C/375°F/gas mark 5 and preheat the grill.

Using a serrated knife, remove the tops of the tomatoes and then carefully scoop out the flesh with a teaspoon. Turn the tomatoes upside down on kitchen paper to drain. Grill the bacon and black pudding until crisp, leave to cool then crumble; leave to one side.

Heat the butter in a heavy non-stick frying pan and sauté the mushrooms for about 2 minutes or until golden brown. Remove and drain on kitchen paper. Mix the crumbled bacon and black pudding with the mushrooms and season.

Place the tomatoes on a non-stick baking tray and fill with the mixture – not too full or the egg will run over the side. Carefully break an egg into each tomato and season.

Cook in the oven for about 9 minutes or until the egg whites are set but the yolks are still runny. Remove from the oven and serve immediately with hot buttered toast.

If you prefer, you can replace the black pudding with a little slice of Dolcelatte cheese.

Smokey bacon hash

This is the kind of breakfast that will last you all day.

110g (4oz) sour cream
2 garlic cloves, roasted (optional)
1 tablespoon chopped parsley
Sea salt and ground black pepper
3 medium potatoes, parboiled and
  grated or finely diced
4 spring onions, sliced
1 Jalapeño chilli, finely chopped
Olive oil, for frying
150g (5oz) smoked bacon lardons

Serves 4–6

Place the cream, garlic and parsley in a bowl. Mix together, season and set to one side. Place the potatoes, spring onions and chilli in another bowl, mix together and leave to one side. Heat a little olive oil in a heavy cast-iron pan, add the lardons, sauté until golden brown, then remove and drain. Add the lardons to the potato mixture and mix well together. Shape into 10cm (4in) rounds.

Clean the pan, return to the heat and add more olive oil. When the oil is hot, gently fry the rounds on each side until golden brown and crispy. Top with soured cream and serve.

Breakfast bruschetta

Try keeping a couple of loaves of sourdough bread in your freezer, if you find it hard to come by. We think sourdough is best, but you can use any other favourite bread.

60g (2½oz) plain flour
Good pinch of cayenne pepper
Sea salt and ground black pepper
2 plum tomatoes, sliced vertically
2 tablespoons olive oil, plus extra for
  drizzling
25g (1oz) unsalted butter
2 medium Portabello mushrooms, sliced
4 rashers smoked streaky bacon
2 slices sourdough bread, toasted
1 tablespoon snipped chives

Serves 2

Preheat the oven to its lowest setting. Over a large plate, sift the flour with the cayenne, salt and black pepper. Dry the sliced tomatoes on a clean tea towel. Heat the olive oil in a large heavy frying pan over a high heat. Coat the sliced tomatoes with the seasoned flour, place in the hot oil and cook gently on each side until the flour is golden. Remove from the pan, drain on kitchen paper and place in the oven to keep warm.

Clean the pan, then return to the heat and add the butter. When the butter starts to foam, add the mushrooms and gently sauté. Season, remove from the pan and keep warm in the oven. Fry or grill the bacon until very crisp.

On 2 warmed plates, arrange the tomatoes, mushrooms and bacon on the toasted sourdough bread. Drizzle with extra-virgin olive oil, scatter over the chives and serve.

Homemade granola

You can buy really good ready-made granola, but this one is so terrific we thought you just might like to give it a try. It will keep for about a month in an airtight jar, so as well as having it for breakfast with yogurt, you can use it for many other things too, such as the granola biscuits below, the French toast on page 16, or as a topping for ice cream or cooked fruit.

250g (9oz) rolled oats
25g (1oz) plain flour
90g (3oz) fresh coconut, shaved
90g (3oz) blanched almonds, halved
90g (3oz) pecan nuts
90g (3oz) hazelnuts, roughly chopped
25g (1oz) sesame seeds
90g (3oz) pumpkin seeds
90g (3oz) sunflower seeds
Grated zest of 1 orange
½ teaspoon sea salt
60g (2½oz) soft dark brown sugar
120ml (4fl oz) hazelnut oil
300ml (½ pint) maple syrup
60g (2½oz) unsalted butter
60g (2½oz) organic dried apricots, chopped

Makes a big jar, about 1kg (2lb)

Preheat the oven to 160°C/325°F/gas mark 3. Line 2 baking trays with non-stick baking paper.

In a large bowl, mix together all the ingredients except the apricots. Spread evenly on to the prepared trays and roast for about 30 minutes or until golden, stirring every 10 minutes. Remove from the oven and leave to cool. Add the apricots and store in an airtight container in a cool place.

Granola biscuits

110g (4oz) unsalted butter, at
    room temperature
90g (3oz) caster sugar
90g (3oz) dark brown sugar
½ tablespoon vanilla extract
1 large free-range egg
150g (5oz) plain flour, sifted with
    ½ teaspoon bicarbonate of soda
180g (6oz) granola

Makes about 24 biscuits

Preheat the oven to 160°C/325°F/gas mark 3. Line 2 baking sheets with non-stick baking paper.

In an electric mixer, beat together the butter, sugars and vanilla extract until pale. Add the egg slowly, continuing to beat until well combined. Add the flour and mix until smooth. Stir in the granola, then drop spoonfuls of the mixture on to the baking sheets. Bake for about 12–15 minutes. Cool on a wire cooling rack and store in an airtight container.

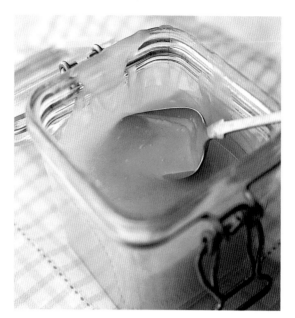

Emma's lemon curd muffins

Emma is the one in my family who is a whizz at making muffins. These have had the seal of approval from her children, Lily and Sam. She often changes the lemon curd to orange curd (and sometimes to marmalade or jam), but the muffins still seem to disappear fast! *Nanette*

Preheat the oven 190°C/350°F/gas mark 4. Place 8 paper muffin cases into a muffin tray.

150g (5oz) plain flour
1 teaspoon baking powder
Pinch of salt
100g (3½oz) unsalted butter
100g (3½oz) caster sugar
3 large free-range eggs, beaten
½ teaspoon vanilla extract
Grated zest of 2 lemons
4 tablespoons good-quality lemon curd
1 tablespoon granulated sugar

Makes 8

Sift the flour, baking powder and salt together and set aside. In an electric mixer on a high speed, cream the butter and sugar until light and fluffy. Reduce the speed to medium and slowly add the eggs, vanilla and zest of 1 lemon. Remove the bowl from the mixer and fold in the flour mixture. Spoon half the mixture into the muffin cases, add 2 teaspoons lemon curd to each and top with the remaining mixture. Sprinkle with the remaining lemon zest and a little sugar. Bake in the oven for 20–25 minutes or until springy to the touch. Cool on a wire rack and and serve warm.

Coffee and walnut muffins

150g (5oz) self-raising flour
Pinch of salt
100g (3½oz) unsalted butter
100g (3½oz) soft light brown sugar
3 large free-range eggs, beaten
1 tablespoon liquid coffee essence
50ml (2fl oz) full-fat milk
150g (5oz) walnuts, roughly chopped
1 tablespoon demerara sugar

Makes 8

Preheat the oven to 190°C/375°F/gas mark 5. Place 8 paper muffin moulds into a muffin tray. Sift the flour and salt together in a large bowl. In an electric mixer on high speed, cream the butter and sugar together until light and fluffy, reduce the speed to medium and slowly add the eggs and the coffee essence until well combined. Remove the bowl from the mixer and fold in the flour. Stir in the milk and the walnuts, reserving some to decorate, and mix until smooth. Spoon the mixture into the moulds, sprinkle with sugar and walnuts and bake for 20–25 minutes or until springy to touch. Cool slightly and serve warm.

Giant apple and cinnamon muffins

These are really worth taking the time to bake and are free from any additives or artificial flavourings. Try changing the apples to pears, or peach slices, and do serve them warm, with a great cup of coffee.

110g (4oz) unsalted butter
2 large eating apples, peeled, cored
 and diced
160g (5½oz) caster sugar
150g (5oz) plain flour
1 tablespoon ground cinnamon
1 teaspoon baking powder
Pinch of salt
3 large free-range eggs, beaten

FOR THE TOPPING
1 large eating apple, peeled, cored and
 sliced into 8
2 tablespoons apple jelly, to glaze
 (optional)

Makes 4 large or 8 small muffins

Preheat the oven to 190°C/350°F/gas mark 4. Place 4 large paper muffin cases into a muffin tray.

Heat 15g (½oz) of the butter in a heavy sauté pan, add the diced apples and 50g (2oz) of the sugar and cook until the apples are soft and caramelised. Spoon the apples into a bowl and leave to cool. Sift the flour, cinnamon, baking powder and salt together. In an electric mixer on a high speed, cream the remaining butter and sugar together until light and fluffy. Reduce the speed and slowly add the eggs. When the eggs are incorporated, remove the bowl from the mixer and, using a metal spoon, fold in the flour mixture followed by the cooked apples. Spoon into the muffin cases, put 2 slices of apple into each muffin and bake for 20–25 minutes for large muffins or slightly less if you are making smaller muffins. Bake until golden brown and springy to the touch. Remove from the oven and place on a wire rack to cool a little. Melt the apple jelly, if using, in a pan or microwave, then brush over the tops of the muffins.

Banana bread

A slice of this with some fresh fruit and a yogurt makes a delicious breakfast. If making this for children, leave out the walnuts.

330g (11½oz) plain flour
1 teaspoon baking powder
1 teaspoon bicarbonate of soda
¼ teaspoon ground cinnamon
110g (4oz) unsalted butter
200g (7oz) caster sugar
2 free-range eggs, beaten
2 large bananas, mashed
110g (4oz) walnuts, chopped
2 tablespoons desiccated coconut

Makes 1 loaf

Preheat the oven to 190°C/350°F/gas mark 4. Line a 23 x 15 (9 x 6in) loaf tin with non-stick baking paper. Sift the flour, baking powder, bicarbonate of soda and ground cinnamon together and leave to one side.
In the bowl of an electric mixer, mix the butter and sugar together until light and fluffy, then slowly add the eggs, continuing to beat. Using a metal spoon, add the flour mixture a large spoonful at a time, and add the bananas. Remove the bowl from the mixer and fold in the walnuts. Pour into the prepared tin and top with the coconut. Bake in the oven for about 45 minutes until golden and cooked through. Cool on a wire rack.

Breakfast Sunday sundae

Make these the previous evening, before you go to bed. In the morning get the coffee on, collect the newspapers and take these out of the fridge – they will make a very happy start to the day.

In 4 tall glasses or 1 large glass bowl, layer the fruit with the granola and finish with the Greek yogurt. Serve immediately, or chill in the fridge overnight and serve the next day.

60g (2½oz) raspberries
60g (2½oz) blueberries
60g (2½oz) blackberries
6 strawberries, hulled
1 peach, sliced
1 mango, peeled and sliced
6 slices pineapple, chopped
4 tablespoons granola
500g (1lb 2oz) Greek yogurt

Serves 4

Sticky pecan buns

Last year in New York we found a wonderful bakery. On the menu were these buns, a cross between a Chelsea bun and a Danish pastry. We decided to have a large bowl of French-style café au lait with a sticky bun. They were so large that they could have easily fed three people. We loved them so much that, on our return home, we decided to perfect these treats and it's great to be able to share them with you – oh, and don't forget the bowl of café au lait. By the way, they freeze very well. *Alison*

FOR THE TOPPING

60g (2½oz) unsalted butter, plus
  extra for greasing
2 teaspoons caster sugar
60g (2½oz) soft light brown sugar
2 tablespoons maple syrup
2 tablespoons liquid glucose

FOR THE DOUGH

15g (½oz) dried yeast
30ml (1fl oz) warm water
75ml (3fl oz) warm milk
15g (½oz) caster sugar
330g (11½oz) plain flour, sifted, plus
  extra for dusting
90g (3oz) unsalted butter, melted
1 large free-range egg, beaten
Pinch of salt
½ teaspoon vanilla extract

FOR THE FILLING

60g (2½oz) unsalted butter, melted
60g (2½oz) soft dark brown sugar
Grated zest of 1 orange
60g (2½oz) pecan nuts, toasted
  and roughly chopped into very
  large pieces

Makes 4 very large buns

Butter a large 4-hole muffin tray. To make the topping, place all the ingredients into a heavy pan and heat over a medium heat until boiling and the sugar has dissolved. Pour into the greased muffin tray and set to one side.

To make the dough, dissolve the yeast in the warmed liquids with the caster sugar (the liquids should be body temperature and no hotter). In an electric mixer fitted with a dough hook, mix the dissolved yeast with the remaining dough ingredients until smooth. Remove the bowl from the mixer, cover with a damp tea towel and place in a warm area such as an airing cupboard. Leave for about 1 hour until the mixture has doubled in size.

Preheat the oven 200°C/400°F/gas mark 6. Turn the dough on to a floured surface and knock back. When it is smooth, roll out into a rectangle about 33 x 15cm (13 x 6in). Brush the dough with the melted butter and sprinkle over the rest of the filling ingredients. Roll up like a Swiss roll and, starting at the short end, cut into 4. Place into the prepared muffin tray and bake for 15–20 minutes until golden. Turn out upside down on to a wire rack, leave to cool a little and serve warm.

If you are planning to freeze these, make double the mixture

Lemon and ricotta pancakes topped with pickled blueberries

These pancakes are much quicker to make than they look on the page.
Children love them – so be prepared to make another batch!

100g (3½oz) wholemeal flour
100g (3½oz) plain flour
1 teaspoon baking powder
Pinch of salt
90g (3oz) caster sugar
250ml (9fl oz) full-fat milk
200g (7oz) ricotta cheese
2 large free-range eggs, separated
1 teaspoon grated lemon zest
Sunflower oil, for frying
Icing sugar, for dusting
Maple syrup or crème fraîche, to serve
  (optional)

FOR THE PICKLED BLUEBERRIES
90g (3oz) caster sugar
90ml (3fl oz) freshly squeezed
  lemon juice
½ small vanilla pod
110g (4oz) blueberries
Small handful mint leaves

Makes 8 pancakes

Ideally, prepare the pickled blueberries the day before you intend serving this dish. Place the sugar, lemon juice and vanilla in a heavy, stainless steel saucepan and slowly bring to the boil. Remove from the heat, leave to cool slightly, then add the blueberries. Pour into a china bowl and cover with baking paper. When completely cold, add the mint leaves and chill in the fridge.

In a bowl, sift together the flours, baking powder, salt and sugar. In another bowl, combine the milk, ricotta, egg yolks and lemon zest and stir together until smooth. Add the flour mixture and mix until smooth. Meanwhile, in an electric mixer, whisk the egg whites until stiff peaks form, then fold into the batter.

Heat 1 tablespoon oil in a large, heavy, non-stick frying pan. Add about 2 tablespoons of the batter to the pan to make a pancake. Cook for about 2 minutes per side, until golden. Transfer on to a plate lined with kitchen paper to drain. Continue to make pancakes in this way until you have used all the batter.

When you are ready to serve, drain the blueberries. Place 2 pancakes on each warmed plate, top with blueberries and dust with icing sugar. If you are feeling very carefree about calories, drizzle over maple syrup, or serve with crème fraîche on the side.

Pumpkin waffles with toasted pumpkin seeds

I first tasted these wonderful waffles in America. Surprisingly they are not dense in texture; they have a nutty flavour and are a terrific treat for breakfast. It's worth having a non-stick waffle maker, because these will become a favourite any-time snack too. *Alison*

Sunflower oil for greasing
110g (4oz) pumpkin purée (fresh or tinned)
60g (2½oz) soft light brown sugar
25g (1oz) caster sugar
1 teaspoon ground cinnamon
Pinch of ground cloves
Pinch of ground nutmeg
Pinch of salt
150g (5oz) plain flour, sifted
1 teaspoon baking powder
½ teaspoon bicarbonate of soda
125ml (4fl oz) full-fat milk
60g (2½oz) soured cream
1 large free-range egg, beaten
½ teaspoon vanilla extract
1 tablespoon dark rum (optional)
40g (1½oz) unsalted butter, melted
Toasted pumpkin seeds, to serve

Makes 4

Grease the waffle maker with oil and preheat. Preheat the oven to its lowest setting.

In a large mixing bowl, combine the pumpkin purée, sugars, spices and salt, and stir in the flour, baking powder and bicarbonate of soda. In another large mixing bowl, combine the milk, soured cream, egg, vanilla and rum, if using. Add the milk mixture to the pumpkin mixture, mix well, add the melted butter and stir.

Pour some of the mixture into the waffle maker until it coats the bottom of the pan and cook for about 3–5 minutes depending on the manufacturer's instructions.

When the waffle is golden and crisp, transfer to a baking tray and place in the oven, leaving the door ajar. Repeat the process until you have used all the waffle mixture.

Place the waffles on warmed plates and serve with toasted pumpkin seeds.

> If you want to push the boat out, serve with crème fraîche and maple syrup.

Smoked haddock fishcakes

Most fishcakes are made by combining fish with mashed potatoes, but these have a much creamier texture because the fish is mixed with a white sauce. We think they are best made with smoked haddock, but of course you can substitute almost any white fish or salmon. Never be tempted to use breadcrumbs out of a packet – they are disgusting. Proper breadcrumbs take only a second to blitz in a food processor. Incidentally, these fishcakes freeze well.

25g (1oz) unsalted butter
25g (1oz) plain flour
300ml (½ pint) milk
375g (13oz) undyed smoked haddock, poached, skinned and boned
3 tablespoons chopped flat-leaf parsley
6 spring onions, chopped
2 tablespoons capers, chopped
1 large free-range egg, hard-boiled and chopped
1 teaspoon English mustard
2 pinches of Cayenne pepper
Salt and ground black pepper
Sunflower oil, for frying

FOR COATING THE FISHCAKES
60g (2½oz) plain flour
2 large free-range eggs, beaten
90g (3oz) breadcrumbs

Makes 4 large or 6 small fishcakes

Line a baking tray with clingfilm or non-stick baking paper.

In a large, heavy saucepan, melt the butter, add the flour and beat until smooth with a wooden spoon. Cook for a couple of minutes over a low heat, then slowly add the milk, stirring all the time to prevent any lumps forming. Remove from the heat, transfer into a large bowl and lay clingfilm or greaseproof paper directly on top of the sauce to prevent a skin forming.

Flake the haddock into large pieces and add to the sauce. Carefully fold in the parsley, spring onions, capers, egg, mustard and Cayenne pepper. Check the seasoning, then spread the mixture out on the baking tray in the fridge for about 1 hour to firm up. Shape the mixture into 4 or 6 cakes.

Place the flour, beaten eggs and breadcrumbs for coating in 3 separate bowls. Coat each cake first with flour, then egg, then breadcrumbs. Heat the oil in a heavy, non-stick frying pan and fry the cakes gently on each side until golden. Drain on kitchen paper before serving on warmed plates.

Long Lunches

We hear a lot about business lunches and ladies who lunch and the old diehard traditional Sunday lunch, but the everyday at-home lunch doesn't figure much in our reckoning, because for most of us, it's usually something left over with a bit of salad or a bowl of soup or just the good old sandwich. Any of these work perfectly but if you're having people to lunch you can't just say, 'Grab an apple and a bit of cheese,' (well, you could, but it would be a very odd cookbook that told you to do that) so we've put together some recipes that we think fit the bill for an eating-in lunch. Some of these recipes also make very good first courses (served in smaller quantities of course).

Crisp and cool cucumber and avocado soup

My friend Gab makes the most wonderful avocado soup; this recipe is homage to his great talent as a home cook. The low-fat crème fraîche makes it beautifully creamy. *Alison*

Place the cucumbers, 3 of the avocados, the lime juice, crème fraîche, spring onions and chilli in a blender and blend until smooth. Slowly add the stock, blend, then pour into a serving bowl.

Taste and adjust the seasoning as necessary. Garnish with the remaining chopped avocado, coriander leaves and lime zest. Serve with warm bread and a green salad.

2 large cucumbers, peeled, deseeded, and chopped
4 ripe Hass avocados, stoned, peeled and chopped
Juice of 2 limes
4–6 tablespoons low-fat crème fraîche
4 spring onions, chopped
1 green chilli, deseeded and chopped
450ml (¾ pint) cold chicken stock
Sea salt and ground black pepper
Small handful of coriander leaves, chopped
Grated zest of 1 lime

Serves 4, or 6 as a starter

Olive oil, for frying
1 large onion, diced
3 garlic cloves, finely chopped
2 sprigs of thyme, chopped
110g (4oz) button mushrooms, sliced
110g (4oz) pancetta, diced
1 leek, sliced
2 celery sticks, sliced
2 large carrots, chopped
1.5 litres (2½ pints) vegetable or chicken
   stock
90g (3oz) orzo or any small pasta
4 medium asparagus spears, cut into 5cm
   (2in) lengths
90g (3oz) fresh or frozen peas
90g (3oz) broad beans, blanched, refreshed
   and skinned
Large handful of flat-leaf parsley, chopped
10 basil leaves, shredded
Sea salt and ground black pepper
4 tablespoons freshly grated Parmesan
   cheese
Grated zest of 1 lemon
Extra-virgin olive oil, to serve

Serves 4

Light vegetable soup with pasta

My husband Bryan makes great vegetable soup – he always adds the zest of a lemon just before he serves it. *Nanette*

Choose a saucepan that is large enough to hold all the ingredients.

Heat a little olive oil in the pan, add the onion, garlic, thyme, mushrooms and pancetta and sauté for about 3 minutes. Add the leek, celery and carrots with the stock and bring to the boil. Add the pasta and simmer for 10 minutes. Add the asparagus, peas and beans and simmer for a further 3 minutes. Add the parsley and basil, season, stir and pour into a large bowl. Scatter over the cheese and lemon zest, drizzle with a little extra-virgin olive oil and serve.

Lobster club sandwich

This is a twist on the classic club sandwich we all love, but just a bit more luxurious. If you don't have brioche, it will still taste good made with an ordinary bread, like granary or seeded brown.

8 slices of Parma ham
12 slices brioche, toasted
4 tablespoons mayonnaise
2 plum tomatoes, sliced
2 Cos lettuces, leaves separated
Sea salt and ground black pepper
1 large Hass avocado, stoned, peeled
  and sliced
2 cooked lobsters, tail and claw meat
  extracted and lightly chopped

Serves 4

Preheat the oven to 190°C/375°F/gas mark 5. Line a baking tray with non-stick baking paper.

Place the Parma ham on the prepared tray and bake in the oven for about 10 minutes, or until crispy, then leave to cool on kitchen paper. Spread each slice of brioche with mayonnaise.

To assemble the sandwiches, place the ham, tomatoes, lettuce and seasoning on 4 of the brioche slices. Top each with a second slice of brioche. Place the avocado and lobster on this and season. Top each with a third slice of brioche, carefully cut in half and serve.

Toasted brioche sandwich filled with smoked salmon and cream cheese

The putting-together of cream cheese and smoked salmon is so corny, but it works well, so why change it?

4 tablespoons full-fat cream cheese,
  at room temperature
1 tablespoon snipped chives
Juice of ½ lime
8 slices brioche
8 large slices Emmenthal cheese
250g (9oz) smoked salmon, sliced
Freshly ground black pepper

Serves 4

Preheat the oven to 150°C/300°F/gas mark 2.

Place the cream cheese, chives and lime juice into a mixing bowl, whisk together until light and creamy, then set to one side.

Toast the brioche and place on a large board. Spread the cream cheese mixture on each slice and top 4 of the slices with the Emmenthal and smoked salmon. Season with black pepper and sandwich together with the other 4 slices. Place on a rack in the oven for 5 minutes, then cut in half and serve.

Asian pear salad

This is fresh tasting, and appetising to look at. For those of you who like serving a first course at dinner, this would work well, served in smaller quantities of course.

2 firm Asian pears
2 ripe Hass avocados, stoned, peeled and sliced
2 bags or 2 large bunches watercress
60g (2½oz) sugar snap peas, cut into strips
  lengthways
60g (2½oz) walnut halves, toasted
12 small new potatoes, cooked and cut in half
Small handful of chives, snipped
175g (6oz) Feta cheese, crumbled

DRESSING

2 teaspoons grain mustard
2 teaspoons white wine vinegar
1 teaspoon caster sugar
2 teaspoons grenadine (optional)
2 tablespoons olive oil
Seeds of 1 pomegranate
Sea salt and ground black pepper

Serves 4–6 or 6–8 as a starter

First make the dressing. In a bowl, whisk together the mustard, vinegar, sugar and grenadine, if using, until the sugar has dissolved. Slowly add the oil, whisking all the time until emulsified, then add the pomegranate seeds and season. Set aside.

Thinly slice the Asian pears and place in a large mixing bowl. Add the avocados, watercress, sugar snap peas, walnuts, potatoes, chives and seasoning. Add the dressing and gently toss together. Transfer to a serving bowl, top with the cheese and serve.

Make double the quantity of dressing and store the remainder in a screwtop jar in the fridge. When you want to use it again, just give it a good shake to re-combine the oil and vinegar.

Asparagus with smoked trout and horseradish dressing

It's vital that the vegetables in this salad are crisp – and just as a reminder, when you have blanched them in boiling water, have a bowl of iced water ready and plunge them into it immediately to refresh them.

12 asparagus spears, cut into 10cm (4in) lengths, blanched, refreshed and dried
90g (3oz) peas, blanched, refreshed and dried
250g (9oz) French beans, blanched, refreshed and dried
12 cherry tomatoes, halved
110g (4oz) baby spinach, any long stalks removed
4 smoked trout fillets, skinned and broken into large pieces
12 quail's eggs, soft-boiled, cooled and peeled
Large handful of chives, snipped
Extra-virgin olive oil

FOR THE HORSERADISH DRESSING
2 tablespoons creamed horseradish
4 tablespoons crème fraîche
6 lemon segments, peeled and cut into 3 pieces
1 tablespoon chopped parsley
Sea salt and ground black pepper

Serves 4, or 6 as a starter

First make the dressing. Mix together the horseradish, crème fraîche, lemon, parsley and seasoning. Spoon into a small serving bowl and set aside.

In a large serving dish, arrange the asparagus, peas, beans, tomatoes and spinach, season and gently mix together. Top with the trout, quail's eggs and chives. Drizzle with the olive oil. Serve with the horseradish dressing.

½ small watermelon, peeled, deseeded
  and cubed
400g (14oz) good-quality Feta cheese, cubed
16 cherry tomatoes, halved
2 Belgian endives, sliced
Small handful of picked flat-leaf parsley
12 mint leaves
12 green olives
Extra-virgin olive oil
Juice of 1 lime
Ground black pepper

Serves 4, or 6–8 as a starter

Watermelon and feta cheese salad

It is a fiddly job getting the seeds out of a watermelon, but worth it, because other types of melon don't work so well in this recipe: the watermelon's crisp, sharp texture is the best.

Arrange the watermelon, Feta, tomatoes, endives, herbs and olives in a serving bowl. Drizzle with the oil and lime juice, season with pepper and serve.

Olive-roasted chicken salad niçoise

Because the dressing is mixed with the chicken while it is still warm, the meat remains moist and full of flavour. This is an any-time-of-the-year salad.

1 medium free-range chicken
1 lemon, halved
2 sprigs of rosemary
4 sprigs of thyme
Olive oil
Sea salt and ground black pepper
2 tablespoons tapenade

FOR THE DRESSING
2 teaspoons Dijon mustard
Juice and grated zest of 1 lemon
1 shallot, finely diced
1 garlic clove, finely diced
½ teaspoon sugar
3 tablespoons extra-virgin olive oil

FOR THE SALAD NIÇOISE
250g (9oz) French beans, blanched
24 cherry tomatoes
12 new potatoes, cooked and halved
Handful of parsley, chopped
8 baby artichokes, drained
2 free-range eggs, hard-boiled, peeled
   and halved
110g (4oz) caper berries

Serves 4

Preheat the oven to 200°C/400°F/gas mark 6. Dry the chicken and place the lemon and herbs in the cavity. Rub the chicken with olive oil and seasoning. Place on a trivet and roast for about 1 hour. Spread the tapenade over the chicken and roast for a further 20 minutes or until cooked through. Remove from the oven and keep warm.

While the chicken is roasting, make the dressing. In a small bowl, mix the mustard, lemon juice and zest, shallots, garlic and sugar. Slowly add the oil, whisking all the time. Season and place to one side.

In a large bowl, combine all the ingredients for the salad except the eggs and caper berries. Season and mix together with some of the dressing.

While the chicken is still warm, remove the meat from the bones, place in a bowl, season and mix with the remainder of the dressing. Add to the salad and toss, arrange the eggs on top and garnish with the caper berries.

Baby artichokes are available in jars from good supermarkets or delicatessens.

Vegetable fritter sandwich with creamed goat's cheese filling

These fritters are so good – children love them, and they go well with a dish of finely sliced tomatoes, simply sprinkled with olive oil and plenty of basil.

250g (9oz) soft goat's cheese
Small handful of chives, finely snipped
150g (5oz) plain flour, sifted
2 large free-range eggs, beaten
225ml (8fl oz) milk
60g (2½oz) Parmesan cheese, grated
200g (7oz) courgettes, grated
200g (7oz) carrots, grated
200g (7oz) parsnips, grated
½ onion, finely sliced
Sea salt and ground black pepper
Good pinch of Cayenne pepper
Sunflower oil, for frying

Serves 4 (makes 16 fritters)

Preheat the oven to 120°C/250°F/gas mark ½ and line a baking tray large enough to hold the fritters with kitchen paper.

Roughly chop the goat's cheese, place in a bowl and whisk until creamy. Add the chives, mix together and leave to one side.

In a large bowl, whisk the flour, eggs and milk until smooth. Add the Parmesan and vegetables and season with salt, pepper and Cayenne. Heat some oil in a large, non-stick frying pan and spoon in the vegetable mixture to make rounds about 8cm (3in) across. Fry until golden on both sides. Remove from the pan and keep warm in the oven. Repeat until you have used all the mixture. Spread the fritters with the goat's cheese, sandwich together in pairs and serve.

Minute steak with red onion and Parmesan

1 red onion, cut into 4 thick slices
Olive oil
Sea salt and ground black pepper
4 large flat mushrooms
60g (2½oz) baby spinach leaves
60g (2½oz) rocket leaves
2 large handfuls flat-leaf parsley leaves
8 x 60g (2½oz) minute steaks
Drizzle of balsamic vinegar
Drizzle of extra-virgin olive oil
Parmesan cheese shavings

Serves 4

Heat a grill pan, drizzle the onion slices with oil and grill, turning, until each side is brown. Remove, season and keep warm. Repeat with the mushrooms, season and keep warm.

Mix the salad leaves together with the parsley and season. Arrange the salad on serving plates with the onion slices and mushrooms.

Season the steaks and sear them on the grill pan for about 30 seconds on each side. Place 2 steaks on each plates, drizzle with the vinegar and oil, top the salad with the Parmesan and serve.

Butternut squash torte

I love the sweetness of butternut squash. I have made this for years – a great alternative to a tart. Serve with crème fraîche made spicy with a touch of sweet chilli sauce if you like. *Alison*

3 large butternut squash, peeled,
  deseeded and cut into cubes
  (prepared weight 1kg (2¼lb)
3 garlic cloves, sliced
2 shallots, sliced
2 sprigs of thyme, chopped
Olive oil
Sea salt and ground black pepper
4 large free-range eggs, beaten
200g (7oz) ricotta cheese
60g (2½oz) Parmesan cheese, grated
4 sage leaves, chopped
Crème fraîche and herby green salad,
  to serve

Serves 6, or 8–10 as a starter

Preheat the oven to 190°C/375°F/gas mark 5. Place the squash, garlic, shallots and thyme in a large roasting tray, drizzle with olive oil, season, cover with foil and roast for about 45 minutes. Remove the foil and roast for a further 30 minutes. Remove from the oven and leave to cool.

Turn up the oven to 200°C/400°F/gas mark 6. Grease a ring mould 18cm (7in) in diameter and 4cm (1½in) deep and place on a large baking sheet lined with non-stick paper. In a large mixing bowl, mash the cooked squash, garlic, shallots and herbs together. Add the eggs, cheeses and sage, season and stir together until well mixed. Spoon into the mould, level the top and bake in the oven for about 30 minutes or until firm to the touch. Remove from the oven and leave to cool. Slide the ring mould on to a serving plate, run a palette knife around the mould and remove. Serve with crème fraîche and a herby green salad.

Fennel, Parma ham and mozzarella salad

This is a very simple salad – if you don't have a mandolin, slice the fennel with a very sharp knife as paper-thin as you can.

2 large fennel bulbs, trimmed
2 buffalo mozzarella cheeses, sliced
8 slices Parma ham, cut into strips
Large handful of chives, snipped
Large handful of parsley, chopped
½ teaspoon marjoram leaves
8 large caper berries
Sea salt and ground black pepper
Juice of ½ lime
Extra-virgin olive oil

Serves 4, or 6–8 as a starter

Using a mandolin, slice the fennel very thinly. Place it in a bowl and add the sliced mozzarella, Parma ham, herbs and caper berries.

Season, and mix together gently. Sprinkle with the lime juice and olive oil and serve.

Serrano ham, plum tomato, fig, mozzarella and basil tart

Although you can buy red onion jam, it goes without saying that homemade is nicer. It also keeps well in the fridge and livens up a cheese sandwich or a bit of cold ham. You can buy puff pastry in a packet ready-rolled, but roll it still more thinly for this tart. If you are expecting quite a few people for lunch, double the quantities given below and make a big square or rectangular tart, remembering that people very rarely restrict themselves to only one slice.

250g (9oz) ready-made puff pastry, rolled very thinly into a free-form circle of about 25cm (10in)
4 tablespoons red onion jam
6 large plum tomatoes, peeled, deseeded and sliced
2 large buffalo mozzarella cheeses, torn into medium pieces
3 figs, quartered
Sea salt and ground black pepper
8 slices Serrano ham
Leaves from 1 small bunch of basil
Extra-virgin olive oil
Green salad, to serve

Serves 6

Preheat the oven to 190°C/375°F/gas mark 5. Place the pastry on a non-stick baking mat or a baking tray lined with non-stick baking paper. Using a fork, prick the pastry to within $1/2$cm ($3/4$in) of the edge and bake in the oven until golden. Remove from the oven and leave to cool.

Spread the pastry base with the onion jam, taking care not to go right to the edge. Top with the tomatoes, mozzarella and figs, seasoning each layer.

Return to the oven for about 10 minutes until the mozzarella melts. Transfer to a serving dish, top with the ham and basil, drizzle with a little olive oil and some freshly ground black pepper and serve with a green salad.

Red onion jam

Sunflower oil
2 red onions, finely sliced
2 tablespoons brown sugar
250ml (8fl oz) red wine
1 tablespoon red wine vinegar

Cook the onions in a little sunflower oil over a low heat until soft. Add the remaining ingredients and cook for 30 minutes until a jam-like consistency is achieved. Remove from the heat and leave to cool. Store in the fridge in an airtight container until needed.

Prawn and ginger stir fry

Once you've assembled all the ingredients, this is a very fast dish to make.

Sunflower oil or peanut oil, for frying
1 walnut-sized piece of root ginger,
  peeled and finely chopped
2 garlic cloves, finely chopped
1 lemongrass stalk, finely chopped
110g (4oz) oyster mushrooms, sliced
2 bok choy, quartered
110g (4oz) sugar snap peas, shredded
110g (4oz) bean sprouts
2 carrots, cut into thin strips
20 large uncooked prawns, peeled
  and deveined
4 spring onions, sliced
1 red chilli, sliced
90g (3oz) unsalted roasted
  cashew nuts
1 small bunch of coriander,
  roughly chopped

FOR THE DRESSING
1 tablespoon light soy sauce
2 tablespoons oyster sauce
1 tablespoon sweet chilli sauce
2 teaspoons light sesame oil
1 tablespoon grated palm sugar
  (if you cannot find this use
  granulated sugar)
Juice of 2 limes

Serves 4

First make the dressing. Combine all the ingredients in a bowl and mix until the sugar has dissolved. Set to one side.

In a large wok, heat a little oil. Add the ginger, garlic and lemongrass and sauté for about 10 seconds. Add all the vegetables and sauté for about 2 minutes. Remove the vegetables from the wok and keep warm.

Clean the inside of the wok with kitchen paper. Add more oil, heat, add the prawns and sauté for about 2 minutes. Return the vegetables to the wok, add the dressing, spring onions and chilli and toss together. Place in a warm serving bowl, scatter over the nuts and coriander and serve.

Mussels Malaysian style

Fishmongers are becoming a rare breed. If there is one in your neighbourhood, treasure him, because he will always tell you when a certain type of fish is at its best, and of course when buying mussels you want them really really fresh.

Heat a sauté pan and dry-fry the cardamom pods and coriander seeds for about 4 minutes, until the coriander seeds begin to pop. Tip into a bowl and leave to cool. When cold, crush using a pestle and mortar.

In a pan large enough to hold all the ingredients, heat the oil, add the shallots and crushed toasted spices and cook for about 1 minute. Add the garlic, chillies, ginger and lemongrass and cook for a further minute. Add the mussels and coconut milk, cover and bring to the boil, shaking the pan occasionally. After about 5 minutes, remove from the heat and drain through a large colander set over a bowl to retain all the cooking liquid. Discard any unopened mussels.

Wipe out the pan, return the liquid and add the sugar and fish sauce, stirring, until the sugar has dissolved.

Place the mussels in a large warmed bowl and pour over the sauce. Add the lime juice, scatter over the peanuts and coriander and serve.

5 cardamom pods
2 teaspoons coriander seeds
1 tablespoon peanut oil
2 shallots, sliced
4 garlic cloves, sliced
2 red chillies, sliced
1 walnut-sized piece root
  ginger, peeled and sliced
2 lemongrass stalks,
  finely sliced
1kg (2¼lb) fresh mussels,
  scrubbed and beards
  removed

2 x 400ml (14oz) tins
  coconut milk
1 tablespoon grated palm
  sugar or granulated sugar
3 tablespoons Thai fish sauce
Juice of 1 lime
60g (2½oz) roasted peanuts,
  crushed
Small handful of coriander
  leaves, roughly chopped

Serves 4

Linguini with crab

We serve this utterly delicious pasta dish with a watercress and rocket salad. It bears emphasising that when you cook the garlic you must do it gently – burn it and you'll have to start all over again, otherwise the bitter taste will spoil the dish.

2 tablespoons olive oil
Sea salt and ground black pepper
200g (7oz) linguini
4 garlic cloves, sliced
8 spring onions, sliced
1 teaspoon prepared English mustard
Grated zest and juice of 1 lemon
250g (9oz) fresh white crab meat
   (frozen will do at a pinch)
2 large handfuls of parsley, chopped
60g (2½oz) Parmesan, grated

Serves 4

Fill a saucepan with salted water, add a little oil and bring to the boil. Add the pasta and cook according to the instructions on the pack until al dente. Meanwhile, heat the oil in a sauté pan, add the garlic and cook gently for about 1 minute. Add the spring onions and sauté for a further minute. Transfer from the pan into a large bowl along with the oil, add the mustard, lemon juice and zest and stir together.

When the pasta is cooked, drain well and add to the mixture in the bowl. Season, add the crab, parsley and Parmesan, toss together and serve.

Seared salmon
with shaved fennel

It's very important that the fennel is sliced as thinly as possible
and a mandolin is best for this, but if you don't have one, use a
very sharp knife – and watch your fingers.

500g (1lb 2oz) salmon fillet, skin on,
  sliced into 8 x 60g (2½oz) escalopes
Olive oil

FOR THE DRESSING
1 tablespoon grain mustard
Grated zest and juice of 2 limes
6 tablespoons extra-virgin olive oil
1 garlic clove, crushed
2 shallots, finely chopped
4 tablespoons chopped parsley
2 tablespoons snipped chives
½ tablespoon chopped tarragon
1 tablespoon baby capers
Sea salt and ground black pepper

FOR THE SALAD
2 fennel bulbs, trimmed
1 red chilli, deseeded and diced
60g (2½oz) walnuts, toasted

First make the dressing. Place the mustard, zest and juice of the
limes in a bowl and mix together. Slowly add the oil. Mix well, add the
remaining ingredients, season and put to one side.

To make the salad, slice the fennel thinly using a mandolin and place
in a bowl with the chilli and walnuts. Pour over half the dressing, toss,
season and transfer to a serving bowl.

Brush the salmon with oil and season. Heat a heavy, non-stick sauté
pan and quickly fry the salmon for about 12–15 seconds on each side
(you will need to do this in batches). Remove the fish to a warm
serving dish, drizzle over some dressing and serve with the salad.

If you can find wild instead of farmed salmon, it is really
worth paying extra for.

Thai chicken cakes
with a pickled cucumber salad

These have such a wonderful fragrant taste.

4 chicken breasts, boned, skinned
   and quartered, about 600g (1¼lb)
   total weight
1 large free-range egg
1½ tablespoons Thai red curry paste
2 tablespoons Thai fish sauce
2 teaspoons caster sugar
Juice and grated zest of 1 lime
90g (3oz) French beans, finely chopped
Leaves from ½ small bunch of coriander
4 kaffir lime leaves, finely shredded
   (optional)
Sunflower oil, for frying

FOR THE DRESSING
150ml (¼ pint) white wine vinegar
60g (2½oz) caster sugar
½ teaspoon ground turmeric
1 red chilli, finely diced
1 garlic clove, finely diced

FOR THE SALAD
1 large cucumber
½ red onion, finely sliced

Serves 4, or 8 as a starter.

First make the dressing by placing all the ingredients in a stainless-steel saucepan and slowly bringing to a simmer. Remove from the heat and leave to cool.

For the salad, cut the cucumber in half lengthways leaving the skin on. With a teaspoon, remove the seeds. Slice the cucumber thinly. Place in a bowl and set aside.

To make the chicken cakes, place the chicken, egg, curry paste, fish sauce, sugar, lime juice and zest in a food processor and blend for about 10 seconds. Remove into a bowl, add the beans, coriander and lime leaves and mix together. Mould into small cakes. A tip is to put a little oil on your hands: this makes them easier to shape. Heat a heavy frying pan, add some oil and fry the cakes on each side until golden. Remove, drain on kitchen paper and arrange on a warm serving dish.

Drain the excess water from the cucumber, add the sliced onion, pour over the dressing, toss and serve with the chicken cakes.

Dinner Time

One of the many nice things about dinner in your own home is that you can do it exactly the way it suits you. Whether you serve it in the kitchen or dining room, or on a balcony or in a garden, it's the food and the people that are important. Making the table look inviting is part of the fun of entertaining, rather like setting the stage before a play, but remember what Lee Bailey (a wonderful southern American cook) said: 'When there's an awful lot going on on the table besides the food, there hasn't been enough going on in the kitchen.' The joys of eating in are the way you set your table, the food you choose to cook, the friends you invite: all are part of the individual way you entertain. You're in your own home, you're eating in – it's all up to you. Some of these recipes also make very good first courses.

Before dinner

If you're not having a first course, you might like to have something with drinks before dinner (not nuts and crisps, but just a little taste of a not-too-filling morsel). Here are some ideas.

Separate the leaves of little gem lettuces carefully, arrange on a dish and put a teaspoon of any of the following inside each leaf:

- Hummous (choose a good-quality ready-made one)

- Smoked mackerel pâté (2 smoked mackerel fillets whizzed briefly in a food processor with a small tub of cream cheese, black pepper, the juice of a large lemon and a tablespoon of horseradish sauce.)

- Hard-boiled egg chopped finely and mixed with finely chopped spring onion, a few finely sliced radishes and chopped parsley, and bound with a little mayonnaise.

Or try some of the following:

Sugar snap peas arranged around a bowl of your favourite dip.

A dish of tiny Italian plum tomatoes or French breakfast radishes surrounding a small mound of sea salt.

Toasted coconut – take the flesh out of a coconut and peel into thin strips. Bake on a tray in a medium oven for 10–15 minutes until gently browned around the edges. Sprinkle with sea salt. Serve warm on a napkin.

A bowl of young broad beans mixed with tiny cubes of salty Feta cheese.

Best cheese biscuits to have with drinks

110g (4oz) plain flour, sifted
100g (3½oz) unsalted butter
90g (3oz) Parmesan cheese, grated
Pinch of salt
Pinch of Cayenne pepper

Makes 30 biscuits

In the bowl of an electric mixer mix the flour and butter on a slow speed until the mixture resembles breadcrumbs. Stop the mixer, add the Parmesan, salt and Cayenne pepper, then continue to mix on a slow speed until the mixture begins to come together into a dough. (Alternatively, rub the flour and butter with fingertips until the mixture resembles breadcrumbs, then mix in the remaining ingredients with a spoon.)

On a floured board, pat the dough into a round, cover with clingfilm and refrigerate for a minimum of 1 hour.

Preheat the oven to 190°C/375°F/gas mark 5 and line a baking tray with greaseproof paper. Roll out the dough to a thickness of about 5mm (¼in) on a floured, cool surface. Cut into discs or any shape you like and place on the baking tray. Return to the fridge for about ½ hour.

Bake the biscuits for 10 minutes or until golden brown. Remove from the oven and cool. Store in an airtight container until required.

Baked sea bass

Some people don't like cooking a whole fish, but it does help to retain all its flavours and it's nice to serve fish this way when you're eating out of doors in the summer. Make sure you surround it with plenty of halved lemons and some fresh herbs. Its simplicity is enhanced by some baby new potatoes coated in butter with plenty of mint – or choose one of the creamier vegetables from Side Orders.

1.5kg (3lb 5oz) whole sea bass
Sea salt and ground black pepper
Lots of fresh dill
4 lemons, sliced
Olive oil

Serves 4

Preheat the oven to its highest temperature. Cut a sheet of foil large enough to make a bag for the fish and place on a roasting tray.

Wash the fish, including the cavity, and pat it dry with kitchen paper. Cover the skin with sea salt. Season the cavity with salt and pepper and then fill it with lots of dill and slices of lemon. Make a bed of dill and sliced lemons in the middle of the foil and place the fish on top. Scatter the remaining dill and lemon slices over the fish and drizzle with olive oil. Bring up the edges of the foil to make a parcel and seal carefully. Bake in the oven for about 20–30 minutes or until the fish is cooked through. Cut open the parcel, carefully slide the fish from the foil on to a warm dish and serve.

Grilled cod with spiced lentils

Any lentils left over from this dish will be delicious the next day, served cold with just a little olive oil poured over them.

Sunflower oil, for frying
1 onion, finely sliced
2 garlic cloves, sliced
2 carrots, finely diced
1 chilli, sliced
1½ tablespoons medium curry powder
200g (7oz) Puy lentils, rinsed well
1 tablespoon mango chutney
750ml (26fl oz) chicken stock
Small handful of coriander leaves,
    finely chopped
4 x 175g (6oz) cod fillets, skin on
Sea salt and ground black pepper
Olive oil

Serves 4

Heat a little sunflower oil in a saucepan and sauté the onion, garlic, carrots and chilli, for a few minutes. Add the curry powder and cook for a further 2 minutes. Add the lentils, mango chutney and chicken stock, bring to the boil and simmer for 15–20 minutes but do not allow to become mushy. Remove from the heat and stir in the coriander leaves. Keep warm.

Preheat the grill. Place the cod on a non-stick tray, pour a little olive oil over the skin, then sprinkle with salt and pepper. Grill for 8–10 minutes or until the skin is bubbling, golden and crisp. Serve on top of the lentils.

Skate with warm flavours of Spain

If you do not like skate, this also works well with cod.

Olive oil, for frying
Sea salt and ground black pepper
4 medium skate wings
90g (3oz) unsalted butter
4 shallots, finely diced
3 garlic cloves, finely chopped
6 tomatoes, peeled, deseeded and
    chopped
2 roasted red peppers, skinned, deseeded
    and chopped
Pinch of saffron
Small handful of stoned black olives
Grated zest and juice of 1 lemon
Large handful of parsley, finely chopped

Serves 4

Preheat the oven to 200°C/400°F/gas mark 6 and place a roasting tin big enough for the fish in the oven.

Heat a little oil in a frying pan, season the skate on both sides, add to the pan and sauté on both sides until golden. Place the fish in the preheated roasting tin and bake in the oven for about 4–5 minutes.

Meanwhile, heat the butter in the frying pan and, when foaming, add the shallots and sauté for about 30 seconds. Add the garlic and sauté for 30 seconds. Add the tomatoes, red peppers, saffron, olives, lemon zest and juice and bring to the boil. Remove from the heat, season and stir in the parsley. Place the skate on a warm serving dish, spoon over the sauce and serve.

Halibut with a sweet basil and mussel broth

4 x 200g (7oz) halibut fillets
Olive oil
Sea salt and ground white pepper
2 shallots, diced
3 garlic cloves, diced
2 carrots, diced
4 celery sticks, diced
1 leek, sliced
24 mussels, cleaned and beards removed
1 glass white wine
450ml (16fl oz) fish stock
Good pinch of saffron
25g (1oz) unsalted butter
Small handful of basil leaves

Serves 4

Preheat the grill. Brush the fish with oil and dust with salt and pepper.

In a large saucepan, heat a little oil, add the vegetables and sweat for about 5 minutes, but do not allow to colour. Add the mussels and wine, cover and cook until the mussels are open. Remove the mussels from the pan, discarding any that are not open, and keep to one side. Add the fish stock and saffron to the pan.

Meanwhile, place the fish under the grill and cook for about 8 minutes. While the fish is grilling, whisk the butter into the broth in the pan. Take the mussels from the shell and return to the pan. Add the basil leaves, check the seasoning and keep warm. Place the grilled fish in deep bowls, ladle over the broth and serve.

Grilled chicken with chorizo and chick pea stew

This is a dish that really needs nothing more than a green salad, and perhaps some chunks of rough bread to mop up the tomatoey sauce.

Olive oil, for frying
200g (7oz) spicy chorizo, sliced
2 shallots, finely diced
4 garlic cloves, sliced
2 teaspoons thyme leaves
400g (14oz) tin chopped tomatoes
1 tablespoon tomato purée
150ml (¼ pint) chicken stock
4 corn-fed chicken supremes, skin on
Sea salt and ground black pepper
2 x 400g (14oz) tins chick peas,
   drained and rinsed
2 large handfuls of parsley,
   finely chopped

Serves 4

In a sauté pan, heat a little oil and sauté the chorizo for about 2 minutes. Add the shallots, garlic and thyme and cook for a further 2 minutes. Add the tomatoes, tomato purée and stock, bring to a simmer and cook for about 15 minutes.

Meanwhile, preheat a grill pan. Season the chicken, brush with a little oil, then grill, skin side down, for about 6 minutes. Turn and grill for a further 3–4 minutes or until cooked through. Remove from the pan and keep warm.

Add the chick peas and parsley to the stew, bring to a simmer and heat for about 3 minutes. Season and stir. Pour into a warm serving bowl and serve with the chicken.

Poussin coq au vin

A variation on a classic dish, the best comfort food. Serve with creamed potatoes or potato gratin. Don't forget to use a very good full-bodied red wine: this makes all the difference to the flavour.

Sunflower oil
4 poussins, cut in half
200g (7oz) smoked bacon lardons
24 baby onions
400g (14oz) button mushrooms
12 garlic cloves, chopped
1 teaspoon thyme leaves
600ml (1 pint) good-quality full-bodied
 red wine
300ml (½ pint) chicken stock
Sea salt and ground black pepper
Beurre manié
Small handful of flat-leaf parsley,
 chopped

Serves 4

Preheat the oven to 160°C/325°F/gas mark 3.

In a flameproof casserole large enough to hold all the ingredients, heat a little oil and brown the poussins all over. Remove them from the casserole and set aside. Add the bacon, onions, mushrooms, garlic and thyme to the casserole and sauté until golden. Add the wine and boil until reduced by half. Add the stock, season, add the poussin, bring to the boil and place in the oven for 1 hour.

With a slotted spoon, remove the ingredients from the cooking liquid and keep warm. Thicken the liquid by stirring in the beurre manié in small pieces and check the seasoning. Return the poussins and vegetables to the casserole, stir, ladle into a warm serving dish, sprinkle with the parsley and serve.

For the Beurre Manié

25g (1oz) unsalted butter, at
 room temperature
25g (1oz) plain flour

Beurre manié thickens an unknown quantity of liquid. You can make it well ahead of time; it keeps for about 5 days in the fridge. In a bowl, mix the butter and flour until well combined and smooth. Form into a neat shape, wrap in clingfilm and place in the fridge until required.

Guinea fowl poule-au-pot style

A twist on the classic Poule au Pot, wonderful on a cold winter's night. You might wonder if the brioche dumplings are really worth taking the trouble to make – they add something special to the dish – though, of course, it's up to you.

First make the dumplings. In a warm mixing bowl, combine the milk, sugar and yeast with a little of the flour. Leave for a few minutes to become frothy, then pour into the bowl of an electric mixer fitted with a dough hook. Add the remaining flour, the eggs, butter, seasoning and chives and beat until the mixture becomes a smooth, elastic dough. Place in a bowl, cover with clingfilm and leave in a warm place until doubled in size.

Meanwhile, make the stuffing. Heat a little oil in a sauté pan and sauté the shallots and garlic for about 1 minute. Add the bacon and livers and sauté for a further minute or until the livers are sealed. Remove from the pan into a bowl. Add the remaining stuffing ingredients, season and mix well.

Fill the guinea fowl with the stuffing and carefully sew each end closed with natural string. Take a saucepan large enough to hold the guinea fowl, vegetables and dumplings and pour in the stock. Add the whole shallots, garlic cloves, bouquet garni and guinea fowl. Bring to the boil, add the celery sticks, carrots and leeks, cover and simmer for about 1 hour.

Meanwhile, roll the dumpling mixture on a floured mixture into small balls. Add the dumplings to the pan and poach for a further 20 minutes or until they have doubled in size.

With a slotted spoon, remove the vegetables and dumplings and arrange on a warmed serving dish. Remove the bird from the pan, slice the meat, add to the vegetables and keep warm. Strain about 1.2 litres (2 pints) of the poaching liquid into a small pan and boil rapidly until reduced. Add the parsley, season, pour into a jug and serve with the guinea fowl, stuffing, vegetables and dumplings.

1 large guinea fowl
2.4 litres (4¼ pints) chicken stock
8 shallots
4 garlic cloves
1 bouquet garni
4 celery sticks
4 large carrots
2 leeks
2 large handfuls of parsley, chopped

FOR THE DUMPLINGS
50ml (2fl oz) warm milk
25g (1oz) caster sugar
15g (½oz) fresh baker's yeast
225g (8oz) strong plain flour
2 free-range eggs, beaten
110g (4oz) unsalted butter
Salt and ground black pepper
2 bunches chives, snipped

FOR THE STUFFING
Sunflower oil, for frying
4 shallots, chopped
3 garlic cloves, chopped
250g (9oz) smoked bacon lardons
110g (4oz) chicken livers, diced
6 sage leaves
Leaves from 2 sprigs of thyme
Small handful of parsley, chopped
2 free-range eggs, beaten
90g (3oz) fresh fine breadcrumbs
½ teaspoon grated nutmeg

Serves 4

Pheasant with roasted vegetables and creamy bacon and corn mash

Cooking pheasant this way ensures it will be tender and full of flavour.

2 oven-ready pheasants
Sea salt and ground black pepper
Olive oil
2 parsnips, cut into chunks
2 medium leeks, halved lengthways
2 red onions, quartered
4 garlic cloves, crushed
1 butternut squash, peeled and cut into chunks
2 teaspoons thyme leaves

FOR THE MASH
200g (7oz) smoked bacon lardons
750g (1lb 10oz) old potatoes, such as Desirée
60g (2oz) unsalted butter
300ml (½ pint) double cream
150ml (¼ pint) milk
200g (7oz) sweetcorn kernels, cooked

Serves 4

Preheat the oven to 180°C/350°F/gas mark 4.

Season the pheasants. On the hob, heat a little oil in a heavy roasting tin and brown the pheasants. Remove the birds, add the vegetables to the tin and sauté until brown. Season the vegetables, return the pheasants to the tin and add the thyme. Cover with a lid or foil and roast in the oven for 35–40 minutes.

Meanwhile, make the mash. Heat a little oil in a sauté pan and cook the bacon until brown; set aside. Bring a pan of salted water to the boil, add the potatoes and simmer until soft. Drain, and rinse the pan. Mash, or pass the potatoes through a ricer back into the pan and add the butter, cream and milk. Heat over a low heat, season and stir until smooth. Add the cooked bacon and corn. Keep warm.

Remove the pheasants from the oven, place them on a warm dish, cover and leave to rest. With a slotted spoon, remove the vegetables from the roasting tin and place on a warm serving dish. Carve the pheasants and place on top of the vegetables. Serve with the mash.

Breast of duck with marmalade-glazed chicory

Duck breasts are now readily available and are easy to cook. The sweetness of the marmalade and the bitterness of the chicory combine to make a wonderful foil for the richness of the meat.

4 duck breasts, skin side scored
Sea salt and ground black pepper
60g (2oz) unsalted butter
4 large Belgian endives, halved
3 tablespoons good-quality fine-cut
  orange marmalade
Juice of 2 lemons

Serves 4

Preheat the oven to 200°C/400°F/gas mark 6 and place a baking tray in the oven to heat.

Season the duck and place it, skin side down, in a cold sauté pan. Place the pan on a high heat and cook for about 5 minutes until the skin is brown and crispy. (This method of sealing the duck will render the fat and give marvellously crispy skin.) Turn the breasts over and cook for a further minute. Transfer to the preheated baking tray and roast in the oven for a further 6–8 minutes. When cooked, remove and leave to rest for 5 minutes.

Meanwhile, heat a large sauté pan, add the butter and when it is foaming add the endives, cut side down. Cook for about 3 minutes on each side until golden. Add the marmalade and lemon juice, shake the pan and cook for a further 5 minutes, or until the sauce is syrupy.

Arrange the endives in a warm serving dish. Slice the duck, drizzle with some of the sauce from the endives and serve.

Roast duck with a hint of Chinese spices

Rubbing the duck skin with Chinese spices gives a subtle flavour. Serve with roast sweet potatoes and steamed Chinese greens.

2 female free-range oven-ready ducks
4 tablespoons Chinese five-spice powder
2 teaspoons Sichuan peppercorns, crushed
4 sweet potatoes, cut into 3cm (1¼ in) cubes
Sea salt and ground black pepper

FOR THE SAUCE
6 large plums, stoned and diced
1 walnut-sized piece root ginger,
    peeled and sliced
150ml (¼ pint) water
1 tablespoon hoisin sauce

Serves 4

Preheat the oven to 220°C/425°F/gas mark 7. Place a rack on a roasting tin large enough to hold the ducks.

Rub the inside of the ducks with the five-spice powder and Sichuan peppercorns. With a larding needle or roasting fork, pierce the skin of the ducks and place them on the rack. Roast in the oven for 20 minutes, then turn the oven down to 180°C/350°F/gas mark 4 and cook for a further hour, draining the fat every 20 minutes or so.

Pour a little of the drained fat into another roasting tin, place in the oven and, when hot, add the sweet potatoes, season and roast for about 50 minutes until tender.

Meanwhile, to make the sauce, place the prepared plums and ginger in a saucepan with the water, cover and stew until soft. Add the hoisin sauce, stir, pass the mixture through a fine sieve and keep warm.

When the ducks are cooked, remove from the oven, cover with foil and leave to rest for about 10 minutes. Pour the sauce into a serving bowl. Carve the ducks and arrange on a warm serving dish. Serve with the sweet potatoes and sauce.

Dave's tournedos of pork wrapped in Parma ham

Dave, we thank you for this recipe because it is so delicious!

6 slices Parma ham
2 x 350g (12oz) pork fillets, trimmed
Sea salt and ground black pepper

FOR THE SAUCE
Olive oil, for frying
2 shallots, diced
150ml (¼ pint) dry cider
150ml (¼ pint) chicken stock
150ml (¼ pint) cream
1 tablespoon grain mustard

Serves 4

Choose a saucepan large enough to hold the pork fillets, fill with water and bring to the boil. On a work surface, lay 2 sheets of clingfilm long enough for the Parma ham and place 3 slices of the ham on each sheet, overlapping the edges of the slices. Place a pork fillet on the ham, season and roll up, covering the meat in the cling film to make 2 tight rolls. Tie each end with natural string and poach the rolls in the simmering water for about 20 minutes.

Meanwhile, make the sauce. Heat a little oil in a saucepan, add the shallots and sauté until soft. Add the cider and reduce by half; add the stock and reduce by half again; add the cream and reduce by half again. Add the mustard, season and keep warm.

Remove the meat rolls from the water and discard the clingfilm. Heat a little oil in a sauté pan, add the ham-covered pork fillets and sauté until crisp. Cut each fillet into 2 and serve.

Roast loin of veal with Tuscan beans

We have used tinned beans for this, because, rather like tinned tomatoes, they are good, but if you prefer, buy the dried ones, soak them overnight and cook them according to the packet instructions before adding to the dish.

1kg (2¼lb) loin of veal
Sea salt and ground black pepper
Olive oil
3 sprigs of rosemary
4 shallots
2 unpeeled whole garlic bulbs,
   halved horizontally

FOR THE BEANS
Olive oil
4 shallots, roughly chopped
4 garlic cloves, chopped
Leaves from 1 sprig of oregano
Leaves from 3 sprigs of thyme
400g (14oz) tin cannellini beans,
   drained and rinsed
400g (14oz) tin borlotti beans,
   drained and rinsed
400g (14oz) tin flageolet beans,
   drained and rinsed
200ml (7fl oz) chicken stock
Small handful of flat-leaf parsley,
   chopped
400g (14oz) tin chopped tomatoes
Grated zest of 1 lemon

Serves 6

Preheat the oven to 200°C/400°F/gas mark 6.

Season the veal, heat a little oil in a large sauté pan and seal the veal on all sides until golden. Place the rosemary, shallots and halved garlic bulbs in a roasting tin, lay the veal on top and drizzle with olive oil. Roast in the oven for 45 minutes (that is, allowing 30 minutes per kg/2¼lb and 15 minutes over)

Meanwhile, make the Tuscan beans. Heat a little oil in a large saucepan, add the shallots and sauté for about 30 seconds. Add the garlic and cook for a further minute. Add the herbs, beans and chicken stock, bring to a simmer and cook slowly for about 30 minutes. Add 1 tablespoon of the parsley, the tomatoes and lemon zest and cook for a further 5 minutes, then transfer to a serving bowl and keep warm.

When the veal is cooked, remove from the oven and leave in a warm place to rest for about 15 minutes. Slice the veal, arrange on a warm serving dish, with the roasted shallots and garlic, pour over a little of the roasting juices and scatter with the remaining parsley. Serve with the beans.

Nic's slow-cooked leg of lamb with flageolet beans

A friend of mine, who is French, cooked this for Bryan and me the first time we had dinner at her home in the South of France. It was autumn, there was a slight chill in the air, but we ate outside anyway. An old wooden table was laid under some olive trees, and she lit an outside log fire. We drank red wine, the children played until they were sleepy, we talked and laughed and ate; we praised her homemade bread, the food, the olives, the fruit, the cheese. Whenever I cook this, I remember that evening. You can't always reproduce the setting – but this recipe works every time. *Nanette*

2kg (5lb) leg of lamb
4 garlic cloves, sliced
Olive oil
Sea salt and ground black pepper
4 red onions, sliced
Plenty of sprigs of rosemary
300ml (½ pint) good-quality red wine
450ml (16fl oz) lamb stock
1 tablespoon redcurrant jelly

FOR THE BEANS
25g (1oz) unsalted butter
4 shallots, finely chopped
3 carrots, sliced
1 large onion, peeled and studded
  with cloves
300g (10½oz) dried flageolet beans,
  soaked in water overnight and drained
1.2 litres (2 pints) lamb stock
Large handful of parsley, finely chopped

Serves 6

Preheat the oven 160°C/325°F/gas mark 3.

Pierce the skin of the lamb with the tip of a sharp knife and stud with the garlic. Heat a little oil in a large, heavy roasting tin on the top of the stove, add the lamb and brown on all sides, then remove from the tin and season. Sauté the onions in the tin until transparent, return the lamb and add the rosemary. Pour over the wine, bring to the boil and reduce by half. Add the stock, return to the boil, then reduce for a few more minutes. Remove from the heat. Smear the lamb with the redcurrant jelly, cover the tin with foil or a lid, place in the oven and cook for about 3 hours.

Meanwhile, prepare the beans. In a large saucepan, heat the butter and sauté the shallots until golden. Add the carrots and cook for about 5 minutes. Add the studded onion and beans, cover with the stock and slowly bring to the boil. Turn down to a simmer, cover and cook for about 1–1½ hours. Season, then drain, retaining the stock.

Remove the cloves from the onion and blend it with half the beans and some of the stock in a food processor until smooth. Stir into the remaining beans, add the parsley and check the seasoning.

Remove the lamb from the oven, leave to rest for about 10 minutes. Slice and serve on top of the beans, drizzled with some of the cooking juices.

Rack of lamb with mint and pomegranate salad

Preheat oven to 200°C/400°F/gas mark 6.

Mix all the salad ingredients together and season well. Cover and place in the fridge until required.

Heat a little oil in a frying pan or grill pan, season the lamb with salt and seal until the fat is crispy and the meat brown. Place in the preheated oven and roast for approximately 10 minutes until still pink in the middle. Remove and leave to rest for 5 minutes in a warm place. To serve, slice the lamb into cutlets, arrange on warmed plates or a serving dish and serve with the salad.

4 x 4 rack of new-season's lamb
Sunflower oil

FOR THE SALAD
4 spring onions, finely sliced
1 garlic clove, finely sliced
Small handful of mint leaves, roughly
    shredded
50ml (2fl oz) extra-virgin olive oil
90g (3oz) chick peas, cooked and
    lightly crushed
Grated zest and juice of 1 lemon
Seeds of 2 pomegranates
Sea salt and ground black pepper

Serves 4

Tuscan lamb

6 lamb shanks
Seasoned flour
Sunflower oil, for frying
24 small shallots
8 baby artichokes, outside
    leaves removed, and
    halved
450ml (16fl oz) white
    wine
10 garlic cloves
1 teaspoon thyme leaves
1 teaspoon rosemary
    leaves, chopped

8 plum tomatoes, peeled,
    deseeded and diced
½ teaspoon saffron
900ml (32fl oz) lamb
    stock
Sea salt and ground black
    pepper
24 small new potatoes
200g (7oz) broad beans,
    shelled
Small handful of flat-leaf
    parsley, finely chopped

Serves 6

Preheat the oven to 160°C/325°F/gas mark 3.

Roll the lamb in the seasoned flour. In a large flameproof casserole, heat a little oil, sauté the lamb until golden, then remove and set aside. Add the shallots and artichokes and sauté for 3 minutes. Add the wine, bring to the boil, deglaze the casserole and reduce the liquid by half. Add the garlic, herbs, tomatoes, saffron, stock and seasoning. Return the lamb to the casserole, bring to a simmer, cover and place in the oven for 2½ hours.

Thirty minutes before the end of the cooking time add the potatoes. About 5 minutes before the end of the cooking time add the beans. Remove from the oven, add the parsley, stir and check the seasoning. Serve in warmed bowls.

Roast venison with a juniper sauce

Marinating the venison is very important for the dish, so plan ahead.

1kg (2¼lb) loin of venison, trimmed
½ bottle red wine
Grated zest of 2 oranges
3 garlic cloves, crushed
2 shallots, sliced
6 sprigs of thyme
2 bay leaves
1 tablespoon black peppercorns,
   crushed
250ml (10fl oz) olive oil, plus extra
   for frying
Sea salt and ground black pepper
2 glasses rich port
300ml (½ pint) veal or chicken stock
30 juniper berries, lightly crushed
25g (1oz) unsalted butter

Serves 4–6

Place the venison in a large stainless steel or plastic container. Pour over the wine and add the orange zest, garlic, shallots, herbs, peppercorns and oil. Turn the meat in the marinade and place in the fridge for 24 hours.

Preheat the oven to 180°C/350°F/gas mark 4. Remove the venison from the marinade and dry with a clean tea towel. Season with salt and pepper. Heat a little oil in a large sauté pan and seal the meat on all sides. Transfer to a roasting tin with a little oil and roast in the oven for about 20 minutes.

Meanwhile, strain the marinade, discarding the wine. Heat a little oil in a saucepan and sauté the vegetables and herbs for about 2 minutes. Add the port and reduce until syrupy. Add the stock and reduce by half. Add the juniper berries, check the seasoning, whisk in the butter and keep warm.

When the meat is cooked, remove from the oven, cover with foil and leave to rest for about 10 minutes. Carve the meat and serve with the sauce. Winter Spiced Red Cabbage (see page 112) and Carrot, Parsnip and Celeriac Purée (see page 114) are great side orders with venison.

1.5kg (3lb 5oz) braising steak (blade or
  chuck), cubed
Seasoned flour
Sunflower oil, for frying
350g (12oz) pancetta, diced
18 baby onions
250g (9oz) button mushrooms
10 garlic cloves
3 carrots, diced
1 medium celeriac, diced
6 celery sticks, chopped
450ml (16fl oz) good-quality red wine, such
  as a rich Barolo
20 tinned anchovy fillets, chopped
2 tablespoons Worcestershire sauce
2 tablespoons tomato purée
1 bouquet garni
600ml (1 pint) veal or beef stock
Sea salt and ground black pepper
Large handful of parsley, chopped

Serves 6

Braised beef with anchovies and red wine

You might think it's a lot of garlic and a lot of anchovies, but this is what makes the taste so gutsy. Serve with creamed potatoes or rice, or just chunks of crusty bread to mop up the juice.

Preheat the oven to 150°C/325°F/gas mark 4. Dry the beef and toss in the seasoned flour. In a large flameproof casserole, heat 4 tablespoons oil. Add the beef and brown on all sides, then remove from the casserole. Add the pancetta to the casserole and brown. Add the vegetables and sauté until golden. Return the beef to the casserole, pour over the wine and reduce by half. Add the anchovies, Worcestershire sauce, tomato purée, bouquet garni and stock. Bring to the boil, season, cover and place in the oven for about 2½ hours. Remove the casserole from the oven and check the seasoning. Discard the bouquet garni and ladle into a warm serving bowl. Sprinkle with the parsley and serve with creamed potatoes and the remainder of the Barolo, plus another bottle, of course.

Simple Suppers

Supper conjures up so many of the things we enjoy most about eating in. It can be a spur-of-the-moment invitation to old friends to take pot luck, or something on a tray while watching that not-to-be-missed television programme; eating early with the children, a meal in the garden in summer, or else some good old-fashioned comfort food while snuggled up in front of the fire with a glass or two of wine. Unlike 'Come to dinner', which suggests something more formal and planned, 'Come to supper' has an easy-going ring to it.

Hearty winter soup

This is one of those dishes that tastes even better if it is made the day before eating, so that the flavours have time to develop. Cavolo nero is now available in some supermarkets.

Olive oil, for frying
110g (4oz) smoked bacon lardons
2 onions, finely chopped
3 garlic cloves, finely chopped
1 leek, sliced
4 carrots, sliced
450g (1lb) cavolo nero or Savoy
    cabbage, shredded
1.8 litres (3 pints) chicken stock
400g (14oz) tin haricot beans, drained
    and rinsed
450g (1lb) spicy chorizo sausage,
    sliced, sautéed and drained
2 large handfuls parsley, chopped
Small handful chives, snipped
Sea salt and ground black pepper

Serves 4–6

Heat a little oil in a large saucepan and sauté the bacon until golden brown.

Add the onions and cook until transparent. Add the garlic and cook for about 2 minutes. Add all the vegetables, stir, pour over the stock, bring to the boil and simmer until all the vegetables are tender.

Add the beans, sausage and herbs, return to the boil, stir and season. Pour into a large bowl, drizzle with a little olive oil and serve with a salad and warm grainy bread.

Use a stock cube by all means if you don't have home-made stock, but be careful with the seasoning, as stock cubes are often quite salty.

Sunflower oil
110g (4oz) smoked bacon lardons
6 celery sticks, sliced
2 sprigs of thyme
900ml (32fl oz) chicken stock
900ml (32fl oz) milk
12 small new potatoes, boiled and halved
3 chicken breasts, poached and cut into pieces
4 sweetcorn cobs, cooked and the kernels
   removed, or 500g (1lb 2oz)
   frozen or tinned sweetcorn
12 spring onions, sliced
Handful of parsley, chopped
Sea salt and ground white pepper
Cayenne pepper

FOR THE BEURRE MANIÉ
60g (2½oz) flour
60g (2½oz) unsalted butter,
   at room temperature

Serves 6

Corn and chicken chowder

Comfort food – need we say more?

First make the Beurre Manié – mix the flour and butter together to make a smooth paste and
place in the fridge until needed.

Heat a little oil in a large pan, add the bacon and sauté until the fat is rendered and the bacon is brown.
Remove the bacon from the pan and drain. Add a little more oil to the pan, then add the celery and sauté
for about 2 minutes. Add the thyme, chicken stock and milk and bring to the boil. Turn down to a simmer
and slowly whisk in the beurre manié in small pieces, making sure there are no lumps. Return the bacon to
the pan and add the remaining ingredients apart from the Cayenne. Bring back to the boil, ensuring that
everything is well heated through. Pour into a large serving bowl, dust with Cayenne pepper and serve.

Sarah's asparagus and pea risotto

I am thrilled that both my daughters are terrific cooks. Sarah, with three teenage children, seems to be constantly cooking for a cast of thousands. This is one of her favourite suppers. She says there is something soothing about standing there, stirring, and drinking a glass of wine, while all around you is chaos. She adds different vegetables and herbs to this risotto, but it's always a taste to enjoy. Being inventive is what home cooking is all about, after all. *Nanette*

About 1.8 litres (3 pints) vegetable stock
90g (3oz) unsalted butter
2 shallots, finely sliced
250g (9oz) arborio rice
100ml (3½fl oz) dry white wine
20 asparagus spears, trimmed, blanched,
  refreshed and each cut into 4
250g (9oz) frozen peas, thawed
Large handful of flat-leaf parsley, chopped
Small handful of mint, chopped
60g (2½oz) Parmesan cheese, grated, plus
  shavings to serve
Sea salt and ground black pepper
Grated zest of 1 lemon

Serves 4

Bring the stock to the boil, then turn down to a simmer.

In a large pan, melt 25g (1oz) of the butter, add the shallots and cook for 2 minutes. Add the rice and stir, making sure the grains are coated with the butter.

Pour over the wine and when it is almost absorbed, add a little of the hot stock. When this is almost absorbed, repeat, stirring all the time, until the rice is al dente and creamy, not runny or dry. You may not need all the stock, or you may need a little more liquid, in which case add a little boiling water.

Add the asparagus, peas, herbs, the remaining butter and the grated Parmesan; stir. Season and pour into a warm serving dish. Scatter with the lemon zest and lots of shavings of Parmesan. Serve with a green salad and a cold glass of white or rosé wine.

Red endive and little brown shrimp risotto

Every year in Venice I order this risotto at one of my favourite restaurants. I am there when the little brown shrimps are just coming into season. Peeling these shrimps would take many hours, so we have adapted the idea by replacing them with potted shrimps, using the butter from the pots in the risotto. You could also buy packets of peeled brown shrimps.

To make a risotto, it's important to get the correct heat. Cook on a medium heat – if the heat is too high the liquid will evaporate rapidly and the rice will not cook evenly; if the heat is too low, the liquid will not be absorbed. You will be able to judge after a few ladles of stock are added. *Alison*

4 pots of potted shrimps, about 300g (10½oz) total weight
1.8 litres (3 pints) fish or vegetable stock
25g (1oz) unsalted butter
2 shallots, finely sliced
1 garlic clove, finely diced
250g (9oz) arborio rice
100ml (3½fl oz) dry white wine
60g (2½oz) Parmesan cheese, grated
Large handful of flat-leaf parsley, chopped
4 red Belgian endives or radicchio, finely sliced
Sea salt and ground black pepper

Serves 4

In a pan or microwave, heat the potted shrimps until the butter has melted. Pour the butter into a bowl. Leave the butter and shrimps to one side.

Bring the stock to the boil, then turn down to a simmer.

In a large pan, melt the unsalted butter, add the shallots and cook for 2 minutes. Add the garlic and cook gently for a further 2 minutes, but do not brown. Add the rice and stir, making sure the grains are coated with the butter.

Pour over the wine and, when it is almost absorbed, add a ladleful of hot stock. When this is almost absorbed, repeat, stirring all the time, until the rice is al dente and creamy, not runny or dry. You may not need all the stock, or you may need a little more liquid, in which case add a little boiling water.

Stir in the reserved shrimp, butter and the Parmesan cheese. Add the parsley and endives and stir, being careful not to break the rice grains. Season, pour into a warm bowl and serve with a green salad.

Farfalle with bacon, peas and cream

So simple, so quick.

Sea salt and ground black pepper
Olive oil
400g (14oz) farfalle
200g (7oz) smoked bacon lardons
3 garlic cloves, finely chopped
200g (7oz) peas, cooked
4 tablespoons mascarpone cheese
Large handful of parsley, finely chopped
90g (3oz) Parmesan cheese, finely grated

Serves 4

Fill a large saucepan with salted water, add 1 tablespoon olive oil and bring to the boil. Add the farfalle and cook according to the pack instructions until al dente.

Meanwhile, heat a little oil in a sauté pan, add the bacon and sauté until crisp. Add the garlic and sauté for about 30 seconds. Remove the bacon and garlic from the pan and drain on kitchen paper. Drain the pasta and return to the pan. Add the bacon, garlic, peas, mascarpone and parsley. Toss and season. Turn into a warm dish, scatter with the Parmesan and serve.

Clams and mussels with spaghetti

Sea salt and ground black pepper
4 tablespoons extra-virgin olive oil
250g (9oz) spaghetti
6 shallots, finely chopped
3 garlic cloves, finely chopped
150ml (¼ pint) dry white wine
1kg (2¼lb) fresh mussels, scrubbed and
　　beards removed
1kg (2¼lb) Venus clams, scrubbed
150ml (¼ pint) double cream
Large handful of flat-leaf parsley,
　　roughly chopped
1 red chilli, deseeded and chopped
Grated zest of 1 lemon

Serves 4

Fill a large saucepan with salted water, add 1 tablespoon olive oil and bring to the boil. Add the spaghetti and cook according to the pack instructions until al dente.

In a deep, heavy saucepan, heat the rest of the oil and sauté the shallots until transparent. Add the garlic and cook gently for a further 2 minutes. Discard any mussels and clams that are not tightly shut, then add the rest to the pan along with the wine. Cook with the lid on for about 3–5 minutes, shaking the pan a few times. Take the pan off the heat and remove the clams and mussels with a slotted spoon into a large bowl, discarding any that have failed to open during cooking. Strain the cooking liquor into a clean pan. When the shellfish has cooled, remove the meat from the shells, reserving a few in the shells for the garnish.

Heat the pan with the strained liquor. Bring to the boil, add the cream and reduce for a few minutes. Add the parsley, chilli and seasoning. Add the cooked spaghetti and shellfish, stir well and pour into a warm serving bowl. Scatter with lemon zest, garnish with the reserved shellfish and serve.

Macaroni cheese

We just had to include this all-time favourite supper dishes for all ages. Our version contains more cheese than many versions – this makes it sumptuous, but if you prefer to use a little less, do.

Sea salt and ground white pepper
Olive oil
500g (1lb 2oz) short-cut macaroni
25g (1oz) unsalted butter, plus extra for
  greasing
600ml (1 pint) milk
25g (1oz) plain flour
350g (12oz) mature Cheddar cheese, grated
200g (7oz) Parmesan cheese, grated, plus
  2 tablespoons for topping
1 tablespoon Dijon mustard
Small handful of parsley, chopped
Good pinch of Cayenne pepper
Good pinch of grated nutmeg
110g (4oz) smoked bacon lardons,
  sautéed, drained and cooled
6 tomatoes, peeled and sliced

Serves 6

Fill a large saucepan with salted water, add 1 tablespoon olive oil and bring to the boil. Add the macaroni and cook according to the pack instructions until al dente. Drain and leave to cool. Preheat the oven to 200°C/400°F/gas mark 6. Butter a large baking dish.

Place the macaroni in a large bowl. Pour the milk into a saucepan, bring to the boil and simmer. In a pan, melt the butter, add the flour and mix until smooth. Slowly add the milk, whisking until smooth. Add the cheeses, mustard, parsley and seasonings and mix. Pour over the pasta, add the bacon and toss until evenly coated. Pour into the prepared baking dish. (At this stage the dish can be cooled, covered with clingfilm and frozen.)

Top with the sliced tomatoes and sprinkle with the remaining 2 tablespoons of grated Parmesan. Bake in the oven for about 30 minutes until the mixture is bubbling and golden. Serve.

Penne with mushrooms and herbs

Sea salt and ground black pepper
Olive oil
400g (14oz) penne
2 shallots, finely chopped
4 garlic cloves, finely chopped
250g (9oz) wild or cultivated
  mushrooms, larger ones sliced
1 red chilli, deseeded and sliced
Large handful of parsley, finely chopped
110g (4oz) Parmesan cheese, grated
Grated zest of 1 lemon

Serves 4

Fill a large saucepan with salted water, add 1 tablespoon of olive oil and bring to the boil. Add the penne and cook according to the pack instructions until al dente.

Heat a little oil in a sauté pan and sauté the shallots for 2 minutes. Add the garlic and cook gently for a further 2 minutes. Add the mushrooms and sauté until soft.

Drain the pasta and return to the pan. Add the cooked mushrooms, shallots and garlic, the chilli, parsley, cheese and lemon zest, toss together and season. Drizzle with a little oil. Spoon into a warm serving bowl and serve.

Parmesan polenta topped with seafood

Sometimes, on holiday, you eat a really simple dish that is easily repeated at home. This is one of them. Each year, when I visit Venice, a pilgrimage is made to the Carampane Restaurant where they serve this very simple dish. *Alison*

Pour the water into a large saucepan and bring to the boil. Pour in the polenta, whisking all the time, then lower the heat and cook and stir with a wooden spoon for about 20 minutes; the consistency should be like that of runny mashed potatoes. Remove from the heat, add the butter and Parmesan, stir, season and keep warm.

Heat a little olive oil in a sauté pan, add the shallots and sauté until transparent. Add the garlic and cook for about 1 minute. Add the squid and prawns and sauté until cooked. Add the chilli, lemon juice and parsley, toss together and season.

Pour the polenta on to a warm dish, top with the seafood, drizzle with a little olive oil and serve.

900ml (32fl oz) water
110g (4oz) polenta
90g (3oz) unsalted butter
90g (3oz) Parmesan cheese, grated
Sea salt and ground black pepper
Olive oil
2 shallots, diced
2 garlic cloves, diced
250g (9oz) squid, cut into rings
250g (9oz) cooked peeled prawns (preferably the large north Atlantic kind, or even, if you can find them, small brown shrimps)
1 red chilli, deseeded and chopped
Juice of ½ lemon
2 large handfuls of parsley, chopped

Serves 4

Baked hake with butter beans

Hake is a much underrated fish, which is a shame, because its firm, white flesh is just right for baking. If you have difficulty finding it, this recipe also works well with cod.

400g (14oz) tin butter beans, drained and rinsed
Large handful of parsley, chopped
1 large red chilli, deseeded and finely chopped
2 garlic cloves, finely chopped
1 shallot, finely chopped
2 tablespoons extra-virgin olive oil, plus extra for brushing
Sea salt and ground white pepper
4 hake fillets, 175–250g (6–9oz) each
300ml (½ pint) fish or vegetable stock

FOR THE SAUCE
1 shallot, finely sliced
125ml (4fl oz) dry white wine
110g (4oz) unsalted butter, at room temperature
Splash of double cream

Serves 4

Preheat the oven to 180°C/350°F/gas mark 4. Place a baking tray large enough to hold the fish and stock in the oven to heat.

In a heavy saucepan, combine the butter beans, parsley, chilli, garlic, shallot and olive oil. Season well and set to one side.

Brush the fish with olive oil and season. Remove the hot baking tray from the oven and pour in the stock, add the fish and bake for 10 minutes.

Place the saucepan with the butter beans over a low heat to warm, stirring every now and then.

To make the sauce, place the shallot and wine in a small saucepan, bring the wine to the boil and reduce to about 1 teaspoon. Turn down the heat to a low simmer and whisk in the butter, a walnut-sized piece at a time. Add a splash of cream, season, pour into a serving jug and keep warm. To serve, arrange the fish and butter beans on warmed plates or on a large serving dish. Hand round the sauce separately.

Charlie's fresh mackerel with a walnut pesto

This was made for a friend who loves mackerel, but couldn't find a recipe he liked: it proved a success. Instead of using whole fish, you can, if you prefer, get your fishmonger to fillet the mackerel. The dish could also be made with fresh sardines, pilchards or herrings. *Alison*

Preheat the oven to 190°C/375°F/gas mark 5.

First make the walnut pesto. Place the walnuts on a baking tray and roast in the oven for about 5 minutes, but do not brown or burn. Remove from the oven, and place on a clean, dry tea towel, fold over and rub to remove the skins. Place the walnuts in a bowl. In a food processor, roughly chop the garlic, capers, shallot, basil and parsley for about 20 seconds. Then slowly add the olive oil. Add the walnuts and process for about 5 seconds. Transfer the mixture to a serving bowl, stir in the lemon juice and zest and mustard and season well.

Preheat the grill and line the grill pan with foil. Wash and dry the mackerel, place sprigs of thyme in the cavity and season well. With a sharp knife, make 3 slashes on each side of the fish on the thickest part. Brush the fish with olive oil and season with salt. Place the fish in the grill pan and grill for 5–6 minutes on each side. The skin will start to bubble and look golden. Serve on warm plates with the walnut pesto. Fennel salad goes well with this.

4 whole mackerel, cleaned
Sprigs of thyme
Olive oil

FOR THE WALNUT PESTO
90g (3oz) whole shelled walnuts
2 garlic cloves
1 tablespoon small caper berries
1 shallot
Large handful of basil leaves
Large handful of flat-leaf parsley
150ml (¼ pint) extra-virgin olive oil
Juice and grated zest of 1 large lemon
1 teaspoon Dijon mustard
Sea salt and ground black pepper

Serves 4

Fish pie

Everyone has their own favourite fish pie recipe, but do try ours – it's simple and old-fashioned. We sometimes add prawns and mussels, and sometimes give it a puff pastry lid instead of mashed potato. Peas with a handful of mint go well with it, or simply cooked baby carrots.

1.2 litres (2 pints) fish stock
250g (9oz) undyed smoked haddock,
   skinned, boned and cubed
500g (1lb 2oz) salmon fillet, skinned
   and cubed
60g (2½oz) unsalted butter
60g (2½oz) plain flour
300ml (½ pint) double cream
Sunflower oil
2 shallots, finely sliced
2 leeks, finely sliced
1 glass white wine
Sea salt and ground white pepper
Large handful of chives, snipped
Large handful of flat-leaf parsley,
   chopped
1 quantity Best Creamed Potatoes
   Ever (see page 117)

Serves 6

In a large saucepan, bring the stock to the boil. Turn down to a simmer, add the fish and poach for about 3–4 minutes. Drain through a fine sieve, reserving the stock.

In another saucepan, melt the reserved butter. Add the flour and cook for 2 minutes; do not brown. Slowly add the hot stock, stirring continuously to prevent any lumps forming. When all the stock is added, cook over a low heat for about 5 minutes, stirring often. Remove from the heat and stir in the cream. Cover the sauce with greaseproof paper and leave to cool slightly.

In a heavy sauté pan, heat a little oil and sauté the shallots and leeks until transparent, but not brown. Add the white wine and reduce until very syrupy. Season and leave to one side.

Preheat the oven to 200°C/400°F/gas mark 6.

In an ovenproof oval dish about 30 x 23cm (12 x 9in) and 6cm (2½in) deep, scatter the cooked fish, shallots and leeks, ensuring they are evenly distributed and season. Add the herbs to the sauce, stir and season. Ladle the sauce over the fish. Top the pie with the creamed potatoes, place the dish on a baking tray and cook in the oven for about 40 minutes, until the top is golden and the filling is bubbling.

Vegetable and mozzarella bake

Watch the aubergines carefully when you are cooking them, because they can burn quickly.

Olive oil
2 aubergines
6 large courgettes, thinly sliced
6 large tomatoes, skinned and sliced
2 tablespoons pesto sauce
Sea salt and ground black pepper
110g (4oz) Parmesan cheese, finely
  grated
2 large buffalo mozzarella cheeses,
  sliced

Serves 4

Preheat the oven to 200°C/400°F/gas mark 6. Brush an ovenproof dish with a little oil. Slice the aubergines thinly and score each slice with the tip of a sharp knife. Heat a little olive oil in a sauté pan and fry the aubergine slices on each side until golden. Do the same with the courgettes. Remove from the pan and drain. Place a layer of aubergines on the base of the prepared dish. Top with a layer of tomatoes and spread these with some pesto. Top with a layer of courgettes. Repeat until you have used all the vegetables. Between each layer, season and sprinkle with the Parmesan. Place the dish in the oven and bake for about 20 minutes. Remove from the oven, top with the sliced mozzarella, then return to the oven until the cheese has melted. Serve hot and bubbling.

Toad in the hole

This is harking back to childhood – winter evening's supper on a tray, watching television. It's one of those dishes that when it's good, it's very very good – and when it's bad, it's horrid. This is very very good.

250ml (9fl oz) milk
120ml (4fl oz) water
110g (4oz) plain flour
4 free-range eggs
Sea salt and ground black pepper
Sunflower oil
12 large sausages (we like
  Lincolnshire, but the choice
  is yours)
2 onions, finely sliced and cooked
  until very soft

Serves 6

Mix together the milk and water. In a bowl, beat the flour and eggs together until smooth. Slowly add the milk mixture, beating until smooth, and season. Cover and place in the fridge until required, preferably overnight.

Preheat the oven to 200°C/400°F/gas mark 6 and place a greased baking tray in the oven to heat. Pierce the sausages, place on the baking tray and cook for about 10–12 minutes in the oven until light brown on all sides. Remove from the oven and leave to cool.

Increase the oven temperature to 220°C/425°F/gas mark 7. Pour a little oil into 6 large, deep Yorkshire pudding tins. Slice the sausages in half, and divide among the tins with the onions. Place the tins in the oven until the oil is hot, then quickly divide the batter among them. Return to the oven for about 15–20 minutes until the Yorkshire puddings are golden brown and risen. Remove from the tins and serve with good gravy.

One-dish chicken supper

We know that when you first see this list of ingredients, you may think, 'too much bother,' and turn the page, but please don't. Take another look – you'll probably already have many of them in your store cupboard. It's not a complicated recipe, we promise, and you'll love the taste. It's a light all-in-one supper.

1 large free-range chicken
250g (9oz) fine egg noodles, cooked and drained
2 tablespoons chopped coriander
Sea salt and ground black pepper

FOR THE STOCK

300ml (½ pint) light soy sauce
450ml (16fl oz) Chinese cooking (Shaohsing) wine or dry sherry
200g (7oz) palm sugar or granulated sugar
4 star anise
1 walnut-sized piece root ginger, peeled and sliced
5 garlic cloves, halved
3 shallots, halved
3 cardamom pods
4 cloves
1 teaspoon Sichuan pepper
1 teaspoon dried chilli flakes
1 teaspoon cumin
1 teaspoon fennel seeds
2 cinnamon sticks
Small bunch of coriander
1 orange, peeled
3 litres (5¼ pints) water

FOR THE VEGETABLES

2 bok choy, halved
8 water chestnuts, sliced
4 carrots, finely sliced
2 Portabello mushrooms, sliced

Serves 4

First make the stock. Place all the ingredients in a large saucepan and bring to the boil. Add the chicken and cook on a gentle simmer for about 1½ hours.

Remove the chicken and set aside. Strain the stock into a clean saucepan, return to the boil and add the vegetables. Simmer for about 4–6 minutes until the vegetables are tender, then add the cooked noodles. Adjust the seasoning as necessary.

Meanwhile, slice the chicken and place into warmed individual bowls or a large serving bowl. Ladle in the stock with the vegetables and noodles. Garnish with the chopped coriander and serve.

Braised ham hock
with a sweet mustard sauce

Cooked this way, ham becomes sweet and tender. We think its perfect partner is Glazed Cabbage (see page 111), but you might feel creamed potatoes (see page 117) are a must.

2 large unsmoked ham hocks, each
   about 1kg (2¼lb)
4 shallots
½ garlic bulb
4 large carrots, cut into bite-sized
   pieces
4 celery sticks, cut into bite-sized pieces
1 bouquet garni
10 black peppercorns
16 new potatoes, cooked and cut into
   bite-sized pieces
110g (4oz) broad beans (shelled
   weight), cooked
Large handful of parsley, chopped

FOR THE SAUCE
3 tablespoons Dijon mustard
2 tablespoons soft brown sugar

Serves 4

Place the ham hocks, whole shallots, garlic, carrots, celery, bouquet garni and peppercorns in a large saucepan, cover with water and slowly bring to the boil. Reduce the heat, remove any scum from the top using a ladle, cover and simmer for about 1½ hours.

To make the sauce, mix the mustard and sugar together in a bowl until the sugar has dissolved.

When the hocks are cooked, remove them from the cooking liquid and slice the meat. Strain the liquid into a clean saucepan, discard the bouquet garni and peppercorns and bring to the boil. Add the cooked potatoes and beans to reheat. Remove them with a slotted spoon when hot and divide among 4 serving bowls with the ham and the other vegetables. Spoon over some stock, scatter with parsley and serve with the sweet mustard sauce.

Little chicken pies

When you say, 'Come to supper', forgetting that you're not going to have much time to cook, these little pies are perfect to have up your sleeve (or, more accurately, in your freezer). They are easy to make on a day when you're in a cooking mood. Freeze them and just defrost, and top with pastry lids and bake when you need them. You may notice that there is an abundance of parsley in the sauce: this works really well, so don't be stingy with it.

350g (12oz) puff pastry
1kg (2¼lb) chicken (choose the cuts
    that you like)
4 sprigs of thyme
2 bay leaves
5 black peppercorns
Sunflower oil
1 large onion, finely sliced
6 leeks, sliced
250g (9oz) oyster mushrooms
60g (2½oz) unsalted butter
60g (2½oz) flour
300ml (½ pint) double cream
2 large handfuls of flat-leaf parsley,
    finely chopped
Sea salt and ground white pepper
1 free-range egg yolk

Serves 6

On floured board, roll out the pastry very thinly and cut into discs to cover the tops of 6 individual pie dishes about 12cm (5in) diameter and 6cm (2½in) deep. Place on a tray, cover and leave in the fridge till required.

Place the chicken in a large saucepan, cover with water, add the thyme, bay leaves and peppercorns and bring to the boil. Poach for about 1 hour until the chicken is tender. Drain the chicken, reserving 900ml (32fl oz) of the cooking liquid, and leave to cool. Strain the cold stock through a fine sieve and set aside. Remove the skin and bones from the chicken, shred the meat and set aside.

Heat a little oil in a pan and sauté the onions until transparent. Add the leeks and cook for a further 5 minutes. Remove the onion and leeks from the pan and place to one side. Add the mushrooms to the pan and cook until tender.

Bring the chicken stock to a simmer in another pan. In a large saucepan, melt the butter, add the flour and make a smooth roux. Slowly add the hot stock, stirring continuously until smooth. Cook on a low heat for 4 minutes. Add the cream, parsley, cooked vegetables and chicken and season. Ladle equal amounts into the pie dishes. You can freeze here if you like.

Preheat the oven to 200°C/400°F/gas mark 6. Place the dishes on a baking tray. Brush the edges of the dishes with the egg yolk and top each with a pastry disc. Brush the top of the pastry with egg and sprinkle with salt. Using a fine knife, make a hole in the centre of each pastry lid, then place the tray of pies in the oven for 25–30 minutes until the pastry is golden brown.

Lancashire hot pot

This is such an old-fashioned meal, harking back to the days when middle neck of lamb was an inexpensive cut. It's one of those dishes that can be nice or nasty: this is definitely nice.

600ml (1 pint) light chicken stock
  or water
25g (1oz) plain flour, sifted
Sea salt and ground white pepper
800g (1¾lb) middle neck of lamb,
  chopped into pieces
Sunflower oil
500g (1lb 2oz) potatoes, finely sliced
1 leek, including the green part,
  finely sliced
2 carrots, finely sliced
1 onion, finely sliced
1 sprig of thyme, chopped
25g (1oz) unsalted butter

Serves 4

Preheat the oven to 160°C/325°F/gas mark 3. Bring the stock to the boil and turn down to a simmer.

Place the flour and seasoning in a bowl, add the lamb and toss to coat. In a large sauté pan, heat a little oil and brown the lamb on all sides. Place a layer of potatoes on the base of a 20cm (8in) diameter, 12cm (5in) deep, ovenproof dish. Add a layer of lamb, then a layer of leek, carrot and onion. Season each layer and sprinkle with the thyme. Repeat the layers until the dish is full, ending with potatoes. Place the hot stock in a jug and carefully pour it into the centre of the dish. Place on a baking tray and cook in the oven for about 2½ hours.

About 30 minutes before the end of the cooking time, melt the butter and brush on to the top layer of potatoes. Sprinkle with salt, turn the oven up to 200°C/400°F/gas mark 6 and leave to brown. Test the hot pot with the tip of a sharp knife: if the meat is soft and the potatoes are golden brown, the dish is cooked. Serve in deep bowls with chunks of bread.

Chump chops
with pea and mint bubble and squeak

Sea salt and ground black pepper
4 large lamb chump chops
Sunflower oil
450g (1lb) potatoes, boiled and drained
250g (9oz) fresh or frozen peas
Small handful of mint leaves
8 spring onions
25g (1oz) unsalted butter

Serves 4

Season the lamb chops. Heat a little oil in a sauté pan or grill pan and seal the lamb on both sides, then fry for about 4 minutes each side. Meanwhile, mash the potatoes, peas, mint and spring onions and seasoning together in a large bowl. Form the mixture into small cakes. Heat a little more oil in a clean sauté pan, add the butter and when it is foaming, add the cakes and fry on each side until golden. Serve the chops and bubble and squeak cakes together, with any pan juices poured over the top.

Gatherings

There are times when you have a large group of people to feed – family or friends – and you need to produce a meal that every one will enjoy (and that usually means people and children of all ages). You also want to cook something that doesn't entail you going demented in the kitchen for hours (I am sure you know those times).

Here are two suggested menus that we think are easy and delicious, and also look especially appetising.

We have taken into consideration that people coming to your home for a weekend lunch (or dinner) often get caught in traffic and arrive late, or will suddenly ring at the last minute and ask if they can they bring a couple of friends (this is particularly popular with teenagers). So these dishes are great hot, warm or cold. They also make great leftovers the next day, so always cook more than you think you'll need. These menus are foolproof, so if your numbers grow just add to your basic ingredients. Don't feel compelled to make a pudding, you can buy really good cakes and desserts, but always have ice-cream in the freezer, together with lots of ice-cream cones (not those nasty pale ones that taste like cardboard, but the thick chunky biscuity ones).

Serve a couple of really good quality cheeses (much nicer than lots of small ones), some great bread and crackers, and a bowl of fruit.

Remember that it's important that you (the cook) enjoy the occasion too.

Apple-roasted ham

Our choice of dishes to go with this would be the Pickled Blueberries (on page 29) and Winter Spiced Red Cabbage with Pears (on page 112). The latter sits very happily in the oven until needed, and can even be made the day before. Creamed Potatoes (page 117) would also go well with it. Serve with a big green herby salad and that's it.

3.5kg (8lb) green gammon
Up to 10 litres (20 pints) organic apple juice,
    such as Bramley (or use apple juice mixed
    with water)
1 large onion, peeled and studded
    with cloves
2 large cinnamon sticks
2 large oranges, sliced
4 garlic cloves
1 teaspoon black peppercorns

FOR THE GLAZE
7 tablespoons redcurrant jelly
2 tablespoons honey
2 tablespoons Dijon mustard
2 tablespoons dark brown sugar

Serves 8–10

Place the gammon in a large container, cover with cold water and place in the fridge for 24 hours. Remove the gammon from the water, place in a stainless steel saucepan, cover with fresh cold water and slowly bring to the boil. Remove from the heat and drain, discarding the water.

Wipe out the saucepan, return the gammon to the pan and add enough apple juice, or apple juice and water, to cover. Add the remaining ingredients, cover and slowly bring to the boil. Turn down to a simmer and poach for about 3–3½ hours.

Meanwhile, combine all the ingredients for the glaze in a small saucepan and warm over a low heat until they melt. Preheat the oven to 180°C/350°F/gas mark 4.

Drain the gammon and leave to cool slightly. Remove the rind and most of the fat and score the ham with the point of a sharp knife. Pour the glaze over the ham. Place in the oven and bake for about 45 minutes until the skin is bubbling and brown, basting with the glaze every 10 minutes. Remove and serve hot, warm or cold.

Rosemary and lemon chicken

This recipe serves 8 but you can easily double or even treble it. Choose one of the side orders or serve with jacket potatoes and a salad of sliced tomatoes and basil.

16–20 chicken pieces – thighs,
  legs or breasts
300ml (½ pint) white wine
Juice of 2 lemons
8 branches rosemary
Sea salt and ground black pepper

FOR ROASTING

3 tablespoons olive oil
4 tablespoons runny honey (acacia
  is the best)
6 lemons, halved
A few branches rosemary
Sea salt and freshly ground pepper

FOR THE SALAD

3 large bags of watercress, rocket and
  spinach salad
A handful of stoned black olives
1 jar sun-dried tomatoes, drained and
  sliced
Your favourite salad dressing
Large croûtons, made from a sliced
  French loaf cut into slices, drizzled
  with oil and sprinkled with grated
  Parmesan then baked in the oven
  until golden and crisp

FOR THE WATERCRESS SAUCE

1 large bunch watercress, very
  finely chopped
1 large tub crème fraîche
Few squeezes lemon juice

Serves 8–10

Put the chicken, wine, lemon juice and rosemary in a plastic container, turn a few times, cover and place in the fridge overnight to marinate.

Preheat the oven to 200°C/400°F/gas mark 6.

Drain the chicken, reserving the marinade, and arrange in a roasting tin or tins. Drizzle with some olive oil and marinade (about 2 small cups for 16 chicken pieces) and the honey. Add the lemon halves and more rosemary and season with salt and pepper. Place in the oven and roast for about 30 minutes until the chicken is brown and crispy. (If you're using chicken breasts, the cooking time will be a little less; while large joints of chicken with the bone in will take longer. Check by piercing with a skewer: if the juices run clear, the chicken is cooked.)

When the chicken is nearly ready, make the sauce, Mix the watercress and the crème fraîche with the lemon juice in a serving bowl and season.

Mix the salad ingredients in a large serving dish, season and toss well.

When the chicken is cooked, arrange on top of the salad leaves with the lemon halves, (they will be nicely caramelised), then add the olives, tomatoes and rosemary branches, pour over the salad dressing and top with the croûtons. Serve with the sauce.

Side Orders

You don't need anyone to tell you that vegetables, when they are at their best, their freshest and their tenderest, should be left well alone. Cooked simply with a few herbs, they are impossible to improve upon. (Think of the new season's baby potatoes with plenty of mint, shining with a little butter and sprinkled with sea salt – wonderful!) However, even with what seems like year-round availability of new-season vegetables from somewhere or other, the really genuine article still has only a short period of perfection. So for the times when vegetables are good but need a little help, we suggest you consult the following pages.

Summer broad beans with spring onions and mint

You must always remove the skins from the broad beans: it's fiddly but worth it. This dish is equally good hot or cold.

3 tablespoons extra-virgin olive oil
1 bunch spring onions, sliced
350g (12oz) broad beans (shelled weight),
   cooked, refreshed and skinned
10 mint leaves, shredded
Grated zest of ½ lemon
Sea salt and ground black pepper

Serves 6

Heat the olive oil in a pan, add the spring onions and cook for about 1 minute; do not brown. Add the cooked beans and stir together until hot. Add the mint and lemon zest, season and serve.

Asparagus and baby broad beans with fresh basil

Summer at its best! This goes well with grilled white fish or chicken, or cold ham.

Sea salt and ground black pepper
25 asparagus spears, trimmed to
   about 10cm (4in)
2 tablespoons extra-virgin olive oil
250g (9oz) broad beans (shelled),
   cooked, refreshed and skinned
30 basil leaves, shredded
25g (1oz) pinenuts, toasted and
   roughly chopped
1 tablespoon grated Parmesan cheese
Juice and grated zest of ½ lemon

Serves 4–6

Bring a pan of salted water to the boil, add the asparagus and cook until al dente. Drain, pat dry with kitchen paper and set aside. Return the pan to a low heat, add the olive oil and, when it is hot, add the remaining ingredients. Return the asparagus to the pan, toss everything together until heated through, season and serve.

French beans and sugar snaps with garlic and parsley

This is so utterly simple, but just serves as a reminder of two vegetables that work well together.

Sea salt and ground black pepper
175g (6oz) French beans
175g (6oz) sugar snap peas
Olive oil
3 garlic cloves, crushed
Large handful of parsley, chopped

Serves 6

Bring a saucepan of salted water to the boil and blanch the beans and sugar snap peas. Drain and set to one side.

Dry the pan, heat the oil in it and cook the garlic for about 30 seconds. Add the parsley, beans and peas, toss together, season and serve.

Runner beans with celery leaves

The taste of celery combines well with beans. Other green beans will work just as well, though the thinly sliced runner has the edge.

250g (9oz) runner beans, topped, tailed, stringed and thinly sliced
Sea salt and ground black pepper
25g (1oz) unsalted butter
Handful of celery leaves, finely chopped
Celery salt

Serves 4–6

Cook the beans in boiling salted water for about 2 minutes, then drain. Dry the pan, return to the heat and add the butter. When it is foaming, return the beans and add the celery leaves. Season with celery salt and ground black pepper, toss together until heated through and serve.

Peas à la Française

This went out of fashion ages ago (isn't it funny how food does that), but as with certain dishes such as roasts and grills, it is worth giving it a bit of a comeback.

25g (1oz) unsalted butter
1 bunch spring onions, chopped
2 small Romaine lettuce, quartered
500g (1lb 2oz) fresh or frozen peas
  (shelled weight)
450ml (16fl oz) light chicken or
  vegetable stock
1 sprig of mint
Sea salt and ground black pepper

Serves 6

First make the beurre manié as described below.
In a large frying pan, heat the butter until bubbling, add the spring onions and sauté until soft; do not brown. Add the lettuces and sauté for about 1 minute. Add the peas, cover with stock, add the mint and simmer for about 10 minutes. To thicken, slowly whisk in small pieces of the beurre manié until the sauce is of the desired consistency. Season and pour into a warm serving dish.

For the Beurre Manié

25g (1oz) unsalted butter, at room
  temperature
25g (1oz) plain flour

Beurre manié thickens an unknown quantity of liquid. You can make it well ahead of time; it keeps for about 5 days in the fridge. In a bowl, mix the butter and flour until well combined and smooth. Form into a neat shape, wrap in clingfilm and place in the fridge until required.

Buttered endive

We have used Belgian endive (the one with the pale green tips) for this dish, but the red one is equally good. This is particularly blissful served with roast duck.

90g (3oz) unsalted butter
4 Belgian endives, halved lengthways
3 tablespoons good-quality runny honey
Juice of 2 lemons
Sea salt and ground black pepper

Serves 4

In a large sauté pan, melt the butter. When it is foaming, add the endives, cut side down, and cook until golden. Turn the endives, add the honey and lemon juice and cook on a low heat until the endives are tender. Season and serve.

12 baby fennel bulbs, halved, or 4 large fennel
  bulbs, each cut into 6
Sea salt and ground black pepper
Extra-virgin olive oil
1 red chilli, finely sliced or 1 teaspoon dried
  chilli flakes
3 large garlic cloves, finely sliced
Grated zest of 1 lemon
1 shallot, finely sliced
Leaves from 1 small handful flat-leaf parsley

Serves 6

Grilled baby fennel
with parsley, lemon and chilli

Baby fennel bulbs are perfect for this dish, so try to get some if you can.
This is fresh-tasting and simple to make.

Bring a saucepan of salted water to the boil, add the fennel and blanch
for about 1 minute. Drain, refresh in cold water, drain again and dry on a
clean tea towel. Brush the fennel with olive oil, sprinkle with the chilli
and grill on both sides until tender.

Meanwhile, place the remaining ingredients in a bowl. When the fennel is
cooked, add to the bowl, toss well and season. Serve warm.

Courgette ribbons with toasted almonds

It's very important in this recipe that the courgettes are decidedly undercooked.

4 large courgettes, topped and tailed
Sea salt and ground black pepper
Handful of almonds, toasted and
  roughly chopped
½ small red onion, very finely sliced
Handful of parsley, chopped
French dressing

Serves 4

Fill a saucepan with salted water and bring to the boil. Using a mandolin, slice the courgettes lengthways as thinly as you can. Blanch the slices in the boiling water for about 2 minutes, drain and refresh in cold water. Drain again and pat dry with a clean tea towel. Place in a serving bowl with the remaining ingredients, season, toss together with the salad dressing and serve.

Crispy courgette pancakes

Have these with plain grills or cold meats.

150g (5oz) plain flour, sifted
2 large free-range eggs, beaten
225ml (8fl oz) good bitter beer
600g (1¼lb) courgettes (about
  4 medium), grated
½ red onion, finely chopped
Large handful parsley, chopped
3 garlic cloves, finely chopped
25g (1oz) Parmesan cheese, grated
Sea salt and ground black pepper
Sunflower oil, for frying

Serves 4–6

Preheat the oven to its lowest setting. Line an ovenproof tray with kitchen paper and place in the oven to warm.

In a large bowl, whisk the flour, eggs and beer until smooth. Add the courgettes, onions, parsley, garlic, Parmesan and seasoning, stir well and set to one side.

In a heavy, non-stick frying pan, heat a depth of about ½cm (¼in) of oil. Drop a tablespoon of the batter mixture into the hot oil and fry gently on each side until golden brown. Remove from the oil and place on the lined tray in the oven, leaving the oven door ajar. Repeat the process until you have used all the batter mixture. Serve hot.

Leeks with parsley and cream

These are particularly good with plain grilled fish and roast meats.

Sea salt and ground black pepper
3 young leeks, including the pale
   green parts, sliced
300ml (½ pint) double cream
Large handful of parsley, chopped

Serves 6

Bring a pan of salted water to the boil and blanch the leeks. Drain, refresh the leeks, drain again and keep to one side. Clean the pan, add the cream and reduce by half. Add the leeks and stir well. Add the parsley, stir, season and serve.

Shredded Brussels sprouts with crispy bacon and toasted pinenuts

Brussels sprouts are not everyone's favourite vegetable – one soggy encounter and you may never want to meet them again. However, cooked this way, they take on a whole new dimension.

60g (2½oz) unsalted butter
175g (6oz) smoked bacon lardons
2 shallots, finely chopped
1 sprig of thyme, finely chopped
750g (1lb 10oz) Brussels sprouts,
   shredded
150ml (¼ pint) light chicken stock
Sea salt and ground black pepper
1 tablespoon pinenuts, toasted

Serves 6

In a large, heavy, non-stick frying pan, melt the butter. When it is foaming, add the lardons and sauté until golden. Add the shallots and thyme and cook until the shallots are transparent. Add the shredded sprouts and stock, season and cook until the vegetables are tender. Drain, place in a warm serving bowl, scatter over the pinenuts and serve.

Purple sprouting broccoli with Parmesan

Sea salt and ground black pepper
250g (9oz) purple sprouting broccoli, trimmed
1 teaspoon aged balsamic vinegar
3 tablespoons grated Parmesan cheese
Extra-virgin olive oil

Serves 6

Bring a pan of salted water to the boil, add the broccoli, return to the boil and cook for about 2 minutes. Drain and place in a large bowl. Add the vinegar, cheese and seasoning and toss. Drizzle with a little olive oil and serve.

Cauliflower cheese

This recipe is really a reminder of a very simple dish. You can steam the cauliflower instead of boiling it, if you prefer.

Sea salt
1 large cauliflower, broken into florets
60g (2½oz) unsalted butter
60g (2½oz) plain flour
600ml (1 pint) milk
110g (4oz) mature Cheddar cheese, grated
25g (1oz) Parmesan cheese, grated
Good pinch of Cayenne pepper
Good handful of breadcrumbs
60g (2½oz) walnuts

Serves 4

Fill a saucepan with salted water and bring to the boil. Add the cauliflower and simmer briefly until al dente. Drain and leave to cool. Preheat the grill.

Melt the butter in a saucepan and when it is foaming, add the flour and stir until smooth. Slowly add the milk, whisking all the time to prevent lumps. Add the cheeses and Cayenne pepper. Check the seasoning. Add the cauliflower and stir gently. Pour into a heatproof dish and scatter the breadcrumbs and walnuts over the top. Place under the grill until golden brown, then serve.

Apple and celeriac purée

This goes wonderfully with game. The addition of apples gives a very smooth texture.

30g (1oz) unsalted butter
2 shallots, peeled and diced
2 garlic cloves, peeled and diced
1 teaspoon of thyme leaves
2 Cox apples, peeled, cored and diced
500g (1lb) celeriac, peeled and diced
150ml (¼ pint) vegetable stock
300ml (½ pint) double cream
Salt and ground black pepper

Serves 4

In a large saucepan, heat the butter and sauté the shallots, garlic and thyme until the shallots are softened. Add the apples, celeriac and vegetable stock. Cover and cook over a low heat until the apples and celeriac are soft.

Add the cream and cook for about 5 minutes, stirring all the time. Season, then place the mixture into a food processor, and process until smooth. Check the seasoning and serve warm.

Glazed cabbage

Perfect with plain grilled meat or simply cooked roasts.

60g (2½oz) unsalted butter
1 large onion, finely sliced
1 large white cabbage, finely shredded
2 sprigs of thyme, roughly chopped
½ teaspoon caraway seeds
1 very large Bramley apple, peeled, cored and
  cut into chunks
300ml (½ pint) dry white wine
2 tablespoons white wine vinegar
Sea salt and ground white pepper
1 tablespoon caster sugar

Serves 4

Preheat the oven to 160°C/325°F/gas mark 3.

In a large sauté pan, heat the butter. When it is foaming, add the onion and cook until transparent. Add the cabbage, thyme and caraway seeds, toss together and cook for 5 minutes.

Spoon into a large, oval ovenproof dish with a lid, add the apple and toss again. Pour in the wine and vinegar and season well. Cover and bake in the oven for about 1 hour until the cabbage is tender. Just before serving, sprinkle with the sugar and glaze with a gas gun or under a hot grill.

Spring cabbage with fennel seeds and nutmeg

Little, pointed spring cabbage is often overlooked. It is inexpensive and full of flavour. Make sure you drain it really well (you can lightly steam it, if you prefer). Don't forget to keep the water for making gravy when serving the cabbage with a roast.

Sea salt and ground white pepper
3 spring cabbages, shredded
60g (2½oz) unsalted butter
1 teaspoon fennel seeds
2 good pinches of grated nutmeg

Serves 4–6

Fill a saucepan with salted water and bring to the boil. Add the cabbage, return to the boil and simmer for about 1 minute, then drain. Dry the saucepan, return to the heat and add the butter. When it is foaming, add the fennel seeds and cook for about 1 minute, but do not brown. Add the nutmeg and cabbage, toss together, season and serve on a warm dish.

> I steam all my vegetables; Alison prefers a quick simmer – we agree to disagree on this point so we leave the choice up to you! *Nanette*

Winter spiced red cabbage with pears

This is a nice change from the usual red cabbage with apple. It reheats well and goes with most meat and game.

Preheat the oven to 160°C/325°F/gas mark 3.

Place all the ingredients except the pears, salt and pepper in a large casserole and leave to marinate for about 1 hour. Stir, season, cover and cook in the oven for about 3 hours. 30 minutes before the end of the cooking time, gently stir in the pears. Serve hot.

1 large red cabbage, finely sliced
2 red onions, finely sliced
300ml (½ pint) red wine
1 cinnamon stick
6 cloves
3 star anise
3 tablespoons rich dark brown sugar
1 tablespoon red wine vinegar
Grated zest and juice of 1 large orange
4 pears, peeled, cored and sliced
Sea salt and ground black pepper

Serves 6

Spinach with coconut milk

Isn't it wonderful that tender baby spinach is now so readily available, often pre-washed too. If you are trying to think of something to have with large prawns this would be great.

Heat a large wok or frying pan, add the coconut milk, curry paste, fish sauce and sugar, mix together and bring to the boil. Add the spinach and stir as the leaves begin to wilt. Transfer to a warm bowl, toss with the chilli and nuts and serve.

4 tablespoons coconut milk
1 teaspoon Thai green curry paste
1 tablespoon Thai fish sauce
2 teaspoons palm sugar or granulated sugar
500g (1lb 2oz) baby spinach, washed
   and dried
1 red chilli, deseeded and finely sliced
90g (3oz) cashew nuts, toasted

Serves 4

Dragon noodles
with a chilli orange dressing

This is great with pork Chinese style or miso-grilled salmon, or just as a salad dish in its own right. It can be served hot or cold.

Sea salt
Sunflower oil
250g (9oz) fresh fine egg noodles
110g (4oz) shiitake mushrooms, sliced
3 carrots, cut into fine strips
150g (5oz) French beans, halved
150g (5oz) water chestnuts, sliced
110g (4oz) cashew nuts, toasted
Large handful coriander leaves
6 spring onions, sliced
1 red chilli, deseeded and sliced
60g (2½oz) crispy shallots (available in
  Chinese supermarkets), optional

FOR THE DRESSING
4 tablespoons light soy sauce
2 tablespoons oyster sauce
Grated zest and juice of 1 orange
1 red chilli, deseeded and finely
  chopped
1 walnut-sized piece of root ginger,
  peeled and finely grated
2 garlic cloves, finely chopped
1 tablespoon sugar
1 tablespoon sunflower oil
1 teaspoon sesame oil

Serves 4–6

First make the dressing. Place all the ingredients in a bowl and whisk together until the sugar has dissolved. Pour into a container and store in a cool place until required.

Bring a pan of salted water to the boil with a little sunflower oil. Add the noodles, return to the boil and cook for about 3–4 minutes. Drain (refresh the noodles in cold water if you are serving this dish cold) and leave to one side.

In a large wok or sauté pan, heat a little oil, add the mushrooms and sauté until soft. Add the carrots and beans and sauté until al dente. Add the chestnuts, cashew nuts and noodles and stir together. Pour the dressing over the salad, toss and serve in a warm dish (if serving warm), topped with the coriander, spring onions, chilli and shallots, if using.

Carrot, parsnip and celeriac purée

Cooked in the oven, these vegetables have a much more intense, sweet flavour.
Serve with lamb, roast beef or roast game.

3 tablespoons extra-virgin olive oil, plus
    extra for the purée
2 garlic cloves
2 shallots, sliced
2 sprigs of thyme
350g (12oz) carrots, sliced
350g (12oz) parsnips, sliced
350g (12oz) celeriac, chopped
Sea salt and ground black pepper

Serves 4–6

Preheat the oven to 190°C/375°F/gas mark 5.

Place all the ingredients in a large roasting tin, cover with foil and roast in the oven for about 1 hour until tender. Place in a food processor and process with a little oil until smooth. Check the seasoning and serve.

Cannellini beans with chilli, garlic and olive oil

This works well with chick peas instead of the cannellini, if you prefer.

3 tablespoons extra-virgin olive oil
3 garlic cloves, crushed
2 red medium-hot chillies, deseeded
    and chopped
1 sprig of thyme, chopped
2 teaspoon white wine vinegar
2 x 400g (14oz) tins cannellini beans,
    drained and rinsed
10 cherry tomatoes, halved
Large handful of parsley, roughly chopped
Sea salt and ground black pepper

Serves 4–6

Heat the oil in a pan large enough to hold the beans. Add the garlic, chillies and thyme and cook for about 1 minute. Add the remaining ingredients, stir together until warmed through and serve.

Classic potato gratin

I have made this dish, which was taught to me by Pierre Koffman, for over 25 years. It's really important to salt the potatoes and leave them for about 10 minutes, as this removes the starch and results in a very creamy finished dish. *Alison*

Butter, for greasing
1 garlic clove
750g (1lb 10oz) Desirée potatoes
Sea salt and ground white pepper
450ml (16fl oz) full-fat milk
450ml (16fl oz) double cream
½ teaspoon grated nutmeg

Serves 4-6

Preheat the oven to 180°C/350°F/gas mark 4. Butter an oval ovenproof dish, cut the garlic clove in half and rub around the inside of the dish. Using a Japanese mandolin or food processor, slice the potatoes wafer-thin. Spread the potatoes on a large tray and sprinkle with salt, tossing well. Leave for 10 minutes.

Meanwhile, place the milk, cream and nutmeg into a large, heavy saucepan over a low heat and slowly bring to the boil, then turn down to a simmer. Squeeze the excess water from the potatoes, and add them to the milk mixture. Return to the boil, reduce to a simmer, stir and season. Pour into the prepared dish and bake in the oven for about 40 minutes or until the top is golden and bubbling. Serve hot. This can be kept warm for about 30 minutes, but does not reheat well.

Corn pie

An American recipe that goes with a lot of things – chicken, of course, and it also cheers up cold meats such as ham.

110g (4oz) unsalted butter, plus extra
  for greasing
1kg (2¼lb) frozen sweetcorn, defrosted
Sea salt and ground black pepper
6 free-range eggs, beaten
Small handful of parsley, chopped
Small handful of chives, snipped
1 red chilli, deseeded and finely
  chopped
250g (9oz) mild Feta cheese

Serves 6

Preheat the oven to 180°C/350°F/gas mark 4. Butter a large ovenproof dish. In a liquidiser, blend the sweetcorn until smooth. Heat a heavy, non-stick frying pan, add the butter and when it is foaming, add the corn and cook for 15 minutes over a low heat. Season, remove from the heat and leave to cool.

When the corn is cold, add the eggs, parsley, chives and chilli and stir well. Pour half the mixture into the prepared dish and evenly crumble over the Feta. Top with the remaining corn mixture. Bake in the oven for about 35 minutes or until golden and puffy. Serve hot.

The best creamed potatoes ever

You may think, 'Who needs it?,' when you see a recipe for mashed potatoes, but although it is such a simple everyday dish, everyone has their own favourite method of making it and this is ours. We think that mashing the potatoes with a potato ricer is well worth while, and we feel justified in saying that this creates 'The Best Creamed Potatoes Ever'. See what you think. Dieters, don't bother to read on...

Sea salt and ground black pepper
1.4kg (3lb) old potatoes, such as
 Desirée, peeled and quartered
450ml (16fl oz) double cream
150ml (¼ pint) full-fat milk
90g (3oz) unsalted butter, plus extra
 to serve
Good pinch of grated nutmeg

Serves 6 or a greedy 4

Bring a large saucepan of salted water to the boil, add the potatoes, cover and simmer until just tender when tested with the tip of a sharp knife. Drain.

Clean the pan, add the cream, milk, butter and nutmeg and slowly bring to the boil. Meanwhile, put the potatoes through a ricer into a bowl. When the cream mixture is boiling, add the potatoes and stir until well combined and smooth. Season, place in a warm serving dish and top with a knob of butter.

The great thing about creamed potatoes is that, apart from being the ultimate comfort food, they welcome any additions: roasted garlic, herbs, grain mustard, cheese – the list is endless.

Miso-roasted butternut squash

Butternut squash always seems like such a strange name for a vegetable. It sounds more like a dance from the 1920s; nevertheless it has a distinctive taste and works well with plain grilled food.

Sunflower oil
2 butternut squash, unpeeled, washed,
 dried and each cut into 4 slices
4 tablespoons red miso paste
2 tablespoons mirin
1 tablespoon caster sugar
2 garlic cloves, finely chopped
1 walnut-sized piece root ginger, chopped
Snipped chives, to garnish

Serves 4

Preheat the oven to 200°C/400°F/gas mark 6. Pour a little oil into a roasting tin large enough to hold the squash and place in the oven to heat.
When the oil is hot, add the squash and roast for about 30 minutes until tender. Meanwhile, in a large bowl, mix together all the remaining ingredients, except the chives, to make a paste. When the squash is tender, remove from the oven and coat with the paste. Return to the oven and roast for a further 10 minutes. To serve, place the squash on a warm serving platter and scatter over the chives.

Chunky potato chips
with sea salt and malt vinegar

There is nothing like freshly cooked potato chips. Choosing the right potato is really important, as is the temperature of the oil. Always blanch the chips, leave them to cool, then refry them. This is vital: the whole process cooks the potato to a crisp and brings out the sweet flavour. Roll the chips in sea salt and drizzle with malt vinegar. When I was a child, my father made great chips; he used dripping in those days, but today an oil that fries at high temperature, such as groundnut (peanut) oil, is fine. Ask yourself: is it the chip or the sea salt and malt vinegar that tastes so great or the combination of all three? *Alison*

6 large Maris Piper potatoes
2 litres (3½ pints) groundnut oil
Sea salt
Malt vinegar

Serves 4–6

Line 2 large trays with kitchen paper.

Cut the potatoes into chips and dry on a clean tea towel. Heat the oil in a deep-fat fryer to 130°C/266°F. Working in batches, fry the chips until slightly golden and soft – a handful at a time is a suitable quantity: do not overfill the basket. As each batch is cooked, remove and drain on the bakings trays lined with kitchen paper. You can do this up to 2 hours before they are required.

For the second frying, reheat the oil to 180°C/356°F. Working in batches again, fry the chips until golden brown. Drain immediately, sprinkle with sea salt and serve with malt vinegar.

Keep a wet tea towel to hand when deep frying – if disaster strikes and the pan catches fire, throw the wet tea towel over the pan and turn off the heat. Do not try to move the pan.

An unusual and delicious variation for vinegar lovers is to sprinkle the chips with malt vinegar before the second frying.

Baked sweet potato with soured cream, palm sugar and crumbled bacon

If you like sweet potatoes, we think this is a great way to enjoy them. Perfect to eat on Bonfire Night or for lunch on a cold winter's day. Serve with something simple – leftover meats, or chicken.

6 small to medium sweet potatoes,
  unpeeled
Sunflower oil
Sea salt and ground black pepper
6 tablespoons soured cream or crème
  fraîche
Large handful coriander leaves
12 rashers smoked streaky bacon
90g (3oz) palm sugar or granulated
  sugar
Dried chilli flakes, optional

Serves 6

Preheat the oven to 220°C/425°F/gas mark 7. Place a baking tray large enough to hold the sweet potatoes without touching in the oven to heat. Pierce the potatoes with a fork. Brush with oil and roll in sea salt. Place on the hot tray in the oven for about 30 minutes. Meanwhile, spoon the soured cream or crème fraîche into a bowl, add the coriander and mix. Cover and place in the fridge.

Under a preheated grill or in a microwave, cook the bacon until crisp. Drain on kitchen paper and leave to cool. Crumble the bacon into a serving bowl, cover and leave in a cool place. To serve, split open the potatoes, season and top with the cream, bacon, palm sugar and chilli flakes, if using.

Roast beetroot

It's fine to used ready-cooked vacuum-packed beetroot for this dish – just steer clear of beetroot packed in vinegar. If you prefer to cook your own, roast small whole beetroot (be careful not to cut the skin while washing them) at 190°C/375°F/gas mark 5 for about 1 hour until tender.

Olive oil
2 shallots, diced
6 beetroot, cooked and cut into
  chunks
Sea salt and ground black pepper
Small handful of parsley, chopped

Serves 4

Preheat the oven to 200°C/400°F/gas mark 6. Place a roasting tin in the oven to heat.

In a sauté pan, heat a little oil and sauté the shallots until transparent. Add the beetroot, season and sauté for about 3 minutes. Turn into the hot roasting tin, pour over a little more oil and roast in the oven for 5 minutes until tender. Toss with the parsley and serve.

Just Desserts

There are many strong-willed people who manage to make their lips frame the word 'no' whenever the word dessert is mentioned – and then there are the others who feel that a little of what you fancy does you good every now and then. Well, the following recipes are for 'the others'.

Baked pears

Choose your pears very carefully for this: not too soft, not too hard, just right. These look nice standing on one of those tall cake stands.

Unsalted butter, for greasing
6 large pears, such as Comice
100g (3½oz) goat's cheese
100g (3½oz) Dolcelatte cheese
6 large vine leaves, optional
1 free-range egg white, optional
Crème fraîche, to serve

Serves 6

Preheat the oven to 180°C/350°F/gas mark 4. Butter a muffin tin.

Core the pears from the base and peel, leaving the stalk on. Mix the cheeses together until creamy and pipe into the pears or push in with the end of a wooden spoon. If using, brush a little egg white over one side of the vine leaves so that they will stick to the pears.

Place the leaves in the muffin tin, place a pear on each leaf and mould the leaf around the base of the pear. Bake for about 30 minutes until the pears are soft. Serve with crème fraîche.

Grilled figs

This is so easy to do; it does not require a formal list of ingredients or method. Just preheat the grill, place the figs on a heatproof tray, cut a cross on the top of each one, open them slightly, sprinkle with a little sugar and grill until slightly soft. They are very nice served with some whipped soft goat's cheese.

Strawberries with a drizzle of balsamic vinegar

There is no real method to this. Just hull the strawberries, cut them half, sprinkle with a little caster sugar, turn them gently with a few torn mint leaves and drizzle with some very good balsamic vinegar. Serve with crispy sweet biscuits.

Chocolate and ginger dessert

Ginger is great with chocolate, and because you can make this dessert two days ahead of time, it leaves you free to cook other things if you are having a lot of guests.

200g (7oz) plain chocolate digestive biscuits
50g (2oz) unsalted butter

FOR THE FILLING
50g (2oz) caster sugar
1 tablespoon ginger syrup (from a jar of
  preserved ginger)
65ml (2½fl oz) water
60g (2½oz) preserved ginger, finely chopped
450g (1lb) bitter chocolate, finely chopped
4 tablespoon brandy
425ml (¾ pint) double cream

Serves 8

Preheat the oven to 160°C/325°F/gas mark 3. Grease a 25cm (10in) spring-release cake tin.

Place the biscuits in a food processor and process to crumbs. Place in a bowl. Melt the butter, pour on to the crumbs and mix well. Press the mixture evenly on to the base of the tin and bake in the oven for about 15 minutes. Remove and leave to cool.

To make the filling, place the sugar, syrup, water and ginger in a saucepan and heat until the sugar has dissolved. Add the chocolate and brandy and stir until the chocolate has melted. Remove and leave to cool but do not allow to set. Whip the cream until it holds its shape, then fold into the cooled chocolate mixture. Pour into the tin, smooth the top, place in the fridge and leave to set for at least 3 hours or up to 1–2 days.

A nutty chocolate cake

This makes a perfect dessert with ice cream or crème fraîche.

Preheat the oven 180°C/350°F/gas mark 4. Grease and flour and line the base of a 20cm (8in) round cake tin.

In a saucepan, slowly melt the chocolate and butter. Meanwhile, in an electric mixer, whisk together the eggs and sugar, then stir in the melted chocolate. Stir in the remaining ingredients. Pour into the prepared tin and bake in the oven for about 25–35 minutes. Cool in the tin before turning out.

200g (7oz) unsalted butter
80g (2¾oz) plain flour, plus extra for
  dusting
280g (10oz) bitter chocolate, chopped
4 free-range eggs
280g (10oz) soft dark brown sugar
1 teaspoon vanilla extract
1 teaspoon baking powder
50g (2oz) hazelnuts, toasted and skinned
50g (2oz) pecan nuts, toasted
50g (2oz) macadamia nuts, toasted

Serves 8–10

Peaches, nectarines and cherries with basil

This is a simple assembly of fruits.

3 ripe peaches
3 ripe nectarines
2 good handfuls of dark red cherries
Small handful of basil leaves, shredded
Caster sugar

Serves 4

Stone and slice the peaches and nectarines. Remove the stalks from the cherries (if you are really feeling good, stone the cherries too). Place the fruits in a bowl, turn carefully with the basil and caster sugar to taste. Leave for about 30 minutes and serve.

Roasted peaches and plums

More of a suggestion than a recipe. You can add other fruits – apricots, nectarines and figs all work well. Cooking fruit this way gives it a mellow, gentle taste.

3 peaches
4 large plums
60g (2½oz) unsalted butter
Few sprigs of rosemary
Dash of brandy or rum
Caster sugar

Serves 4

Preheat the oven to its highest temperature. Cut the fruit in half and remove the stones. Place the fruit in a shallow, ovenproof dish, cut side up, and add the diced butter, rosemary and brandy or rum. Sprinkle with sugar to taste and toss gently. Roast for about 12–15 minutes until just soft and the tops are slightly brown. Serve with the juices drizzled over.

Quick and easy raspberry soufflés

This is a soufflé that can't fail – it's foolproof. The mixture can be made hours ahead, if you wish, and the whisked egg whites added just before baking. If you want to make pretty stripes on the soufflés, use a clean paintbrush to paint lines of raspberry purée on the inside of the greased moulds before spooning the mixture in. Raspberry purée is easily made by whizzing up a couple of punnets of raspberries in the food processor.

Preheat the oven to 190°C/375°F/gas mark 5. Prepare 6 moulds about 8cm (3in) in diameter and 5.5cm (2in) in depth by brushing them with a little melted butter and sprinkling with caster sugar. Place on a baking tray and leave to one side.

Place the raspberry purée in a saucepan and slowly bring to the boil. Mix the arrowroot with a little water until smooth. Remove the boiling purée from the heat, whisk in the arrowroot and stir until thick. Leave to cool.

Whisk the egg whites to stiff peaks and gradually whisk in the sugar until stiff and glossy. Beat one third of the egg white mixture into the cooled purée, then carefully fold in the remainder. Spoon into the prepared moulds, smooth the tops and bake for about 8–10 minutes until the soufflés are risen. Serve immediately.

Unsalted butter, melted
300ml (½ pint) raspberry purée
20g (¾oz) arrowroot
6 free-range egg whites
100g (3½oz) caster sugar, plus extra for
   the moulds

Serves 6

Grown-up jelly and ice-cream

Obviously fresh fruit is best for this, but frozen berries also work wonderfully. Some packets consist only of dark fruits (blackberries, blackcurrants, black cherries and so on) and others only of red fruits. If making the terrine with dark fruit, use blackcurrant jelly instead of raspberry. Remember to give your jelly and fruit a quick stir when it's been in the fridge for about 5 or 10 minutes – this ensures that the fruit isn't all sitting on the bottom.

125g (4½oz) punnet strawberries, hulled and halved
2 x 125g (4½oz) punnets raspberries
2 x 125g (4½oz) punnets blackberries
2 x 125g (4½oz) punnets blueberries
2 x 135g (4¾oz) packets raspberry jelly
Ice-cream or whipped cream, to serve

Serves 8–10

Line a 28 x 7 x 7cm (11 x 3 x 3in) terrine with clingfilm. Place all the berries in the terrine. Make up the jelly following the pack instructions and leave to cool.

When the jelly has cooled, pour it into the tin. Cover and place in the fridge to set, stirring once after 5–10 minutes.

When the jelly is fully set, turn it out on to a serving dish and serve with ice cream or whipped cream.

Lemon and lime pots

Do give these a try – they are so easy to make and they taste wonderful.

900ml (1½ pints) double cream
150g (5oz) caster sugar
Grated zest of 2 limes
Juice of 3 lemons
Red fruit, edible flowers or herbs, to garnish

Serves 6

In a heavy saucepan, bring the cream slowly to the boil with the sugar and lime zest. Remove from the heat and leave to infuse for about 10 minutes.

Whisk the lemon juice into the cream and pass through a sieve. Pour into 6 pots and leave to set in the fridge overnight. To serve, garnish with any red fruit or a few edible flowers or herbs.

If you prefer your meringues more cooked on the inside, cook them for another half an hour or so.

Giant clouds

You can buy good meringues everywhere, but they are never quite as nice as homemade. These are to have with ice cream, or make them smaller and sandwich them together with thickly whipped cream. The crystallised violets are a bit of fun.

Preheat the oven to its lowest setting. Line a baking sheet with non-stick baking paper.

In an electric mixer, whisk the egg whites until stiff. Slowly add the sugar, continuing to beat until stiff and glossy.

Using a large spoon, spoon the meringues into 6 well-spaced piles on the prepared baking sheet. Sprinkle the top of each one with nuts and violets. Bake for about 1¹/₂–2 hours until the outside is crisp but the inside is still soft. Cool, then store in an airtight container.

6 free-range egg whites
400g (14oz) caster sugar
Pistachio nuts
Flaked almonds
Crystallised violets

Serves 6

Knickerbocker glories

I admit it, I have a thing about knickerbocker glories – perhaps I'm nostalgic for those old American movies where a girl sat on a drugstore high stool, gazing at a boy over the top of a glass filled with calorific goodies. Whatever the reason, I love them, so I had to include them. *Alison*

1 x 135g (4¾oz) packet raspberry jelly

FOR THE CHOCOLATE MOUSSE
40g (1½oz) glucose powder
60ml (2½fl oz) water
1 gelatine leaf, soaked in cold water
200g (7oz) bitter chocolate, chopped
400ml (14fl oz) double cream

TO FINISH
1litre (2 pint) tub strawberry and vanilla
   ice cream
400ml (14fl oz) double cream, whipped
125g (4½oz) punnet each of strawberries,
   raspberries and blackberries

Serves 6

Make up the jelly to the packet instructions and divide equally between 6 tall glasses. Leave to set.

Meanwhile, make the chocolate mousse. Place the glucose and water in a saucepan and heat until the glucose has dissolved. Squeeze the excess water from the gelatin, add to the hot mixture and stir. Pour over the chocolate in a bowl and whisk until the chocolate has melted and is smooth. Leave to cool.

Whip the cream until it just holds it shape, then stir into the cooled chocolate mixture. Spoon carefully or pipe into the glasses. Cover and place in the fridge until required.

To serve, add scoops of ice cream to each glass and top with whipped cream and fruit.

Passion fruit and coconut cheesecake

This is truly a great-tasting cheesecake.

50g (2oz) desiccated coconut
300g (10½oz) ginger biscuits
100g (3½oz) unsalted butter

FOR THE FILLING
150ml (¼ pint) coconut milk
5 gelatine leaves
6 large passion fruit
500ml (18fl oz) double cream
300g (10½oz) cream cheese
60g (2½oz) caster sugar

FOR THE TOP
2 passion fruit
Shaved fresh coconut (optional
   but adds the final touch if you
   have time)

Serves 8

Preheat the oven to 180°C/350°F/gas mark 4. Grease a 25cm (10in) spring-release cake tin.

Place the coconut and biscuits in a food processor and process to medium crumbs. Place in a bowl. Melt the butter, pour on to the crumbs and mix well. Press evenly on to the base of the tin and bake in the oven for 10 minutes. Remove and leave to cool.

To make the filling, warm the coconut milk, add the gelatine and leave to dissolve. Cut the passion fruit in half, remove the flesh into a bowl and leave to one side. Lightly whip the cream. Cream the cheese with the sugar until smooth, then gradually beat in the cooled coconut milk. Fold in the cream and passion fruit. Pour on to the prepared base, cover and leave in the fridge for about 2 hours to set.

To finish, remove the cheesecake from the tin and place on a serving plate. Cut the passion fruit in half and scoop out the flesh to form an even layer over the top of the cheesecake. Scatter with the coconut shavings, if using.

Pinenut tart

This is one of our favourite tarts. Try it with a scoop of Olive Oil Ice cream (see page 144).

1 quantity Sweet Crust Pastry (see opposite)

FOR THE FILLING
6 free-range eggs
300g (10½oz) soft dark brown sugar
1 teaspoon vanilla extract
150g (5oz) unsalted butter
200g (7oz) golden syrup
300g (10½oz) pinenuts, toasted

Serves 8

Line a 20cm (8in) tart tin with the pastry. Prick the bottom with a fork. Place in the fridge for about 1 hour.

Preheat the oven to 180°C/350°F/gas mark 4. Line the pastry case with foil, cover with baking beans and bake for about 25 minutes. Remove the foil and beans and bake for a further 7–8 minutes, until golden. Remove the pastry case from the oven and lower the temperature to 160°C/325°F/gas mark 3.

To make the filling, whisk the eggs, sugar and vanilla together using an electric mixer. In a saucepan, melt the butter and syrup, then pour into the egg mixture and whisk until smooth. Scatter the pinenuts over the the pastry case, pour in the mixture and bake for about 30–40 minutes or until the firm to the touch. Cool on a rack before serving.

Prune tart

Don't be put off by the name – this is the most delicious moist tart, great served warm with a scoop of Prune and Armagnac Ice Cream (see page 146). It's best eaten on the day of making.

1 quantity Sweet Crust Pastry (see below)

FOR THE FILLING
2 tea bags
200g (7oz) prunes, stoned
600ml (1 pint) crème fraîche
1 teaspoon ground cinnamon
Grated zest of 3 oranges
9 free-range egg yolks
175g (6oz) caster sugar
60g (2½oz) plain flour

Serves 6–8

Place the tea bags and prunes in a bowl and cover with plenty of boiling water. Leave for about 2 hours until the prunes are plump. Drain, discarding the tea bags and reserving the liquid. Meanwhile, line a 20cm (8in) tart tin at least 5cm (2in) deep with the pastry. Prick the bottom with a fork and place in the fridge for about 1 hour.

Preheat the oven to 180°C/350°F/gas mark 4. Line the pastry case with foil, cover with baking beans and bake for 25 minutes. Remove the foil and beans and bake for a further 7–8 minutes, until golden. Remove from the oven and lower the temperature to 160°C/325°F/gas mark 3. In a heavy pan, bring the crème fraîche, 3 tablespoons of the prune liquid, cinnamon and orange zest to the boil. Whisk the egg yolks, sugar and flour in an electric mixer until light and fluffy. Reduce the speed and pour in the crème fraîche mixture, beating until the ingredients are well combined. Place the prunes on the base of the pastry case. Pour the custard mixture over and bake for about 35–40 minutes until just set. Cool on a wire rack. Serve at room temperature or warmed through in the oven.

Sweet crust pastry

Most of us buy frozen pastry, but we thought we'd include our favourite recipe for making sweet tart cases. You can add flavourings to the flour – try grated nutmeg, grated orange zest or ground cinnamon.

250g (9oz) plain flour, plus extra for dusting
25g (1oz) ground almonds
140g (4½oz) unsalted butter
100g (3½oz) icing sugar, sifted
1 free-range egg

Lines a 20cm (8in) round tart tin.

Sift the flour and ground almonds together. In an electric mixer, beat the butter and icing sugar until light and fluffy. Beat in the egg. Add the flour and beat into the mixture.

Place the dough on a floured board and knead until smooth. Wrap in clingfilm and place in the fridge for at least 2 hours, or until required.

Rhubarb and almond cake

This wonderful, moist cake has two personalities. It's great both for tea and served warm as a dessert with crème fraîche. If you can find champagne rhubarb, all the better.

In a large bowl, toss the rhubarb and demerara sugar together. Leave in a cool place for about 2 hours. Preheat the oven to 180°C/350°F/gas mark 4. Butter a spring-release cake tin and line the bottom with non-stick baking paper.

In an electric mixer whisk the butter and caster sugar together on the highest speed, until light and creamy. Reduce the speed to medium and add the eggs one at time, so that the mixture does not curdle. (If it does, just add a little of the flour and beat.) Stir in the flour, ground almonds and 60g (2½oz) of the flaked almonds, mixing until smooth. Add 2 tablespoons of the rhubarb and gently fold in. Pour the cake mixture into the prepared tin, pile the remaining rhubarb in the centre, sprinkle the remaining flaked almonds on top and bake in the oven for 45 minutes. Turn the heat down to 150°C/300°F/gas mark 2 and bake for a further 40–45 minutes.

Remove the cake from the oven, leave in the tin for 10 minutes, then turn out on to a wire cooling rack. Serve cold.

650g (1lb 7oz) rhubarb, strings removed and
    cut into small chunks
60g (2½oz) demerara sugar
175g (6oz) unsalted butter, at room
    temperature, plus extra for greasing
175g (6oz) caster sugar
3 large free-range eggs
125g (4½oz) self-raising flour
60g (2½oz) ground almonds
90g (3oz) flaked almonds

Serves 10

Almond and orange cake

The nice thing about serving cake as a dessert is that if there is any left over, you can have it for tea. This tastes good with crème fraîche.

2 large oranges
60g (2½oz) self-raising flour, plus
　extra for dusting
2 teaspoons baking powder
125g (4½oz) unsalted butter, plus
　extra for greasing
200g (7oz) caster sugar
5 large free-range eggs, beaten
225g (8oz) ground almonds

FOR THE SYRUP
200g (7oz) caster sugar
300ml (½ pint) orange juice

Serves 8-10

Place the oranges in a saucepan, cover with water and simmer for 1½–2 hours or until tender. Drain and leave to cool. Cut into quarters and discard the pips. Place in a food processor and process until smooth. Transfer to a bowl.

Preheat the oven to 180°C/350°F/gas mark 4. Grease and flour a 23cm (9in) spring-release cake tin.

Sift together the baking powder and flour; leave to one side. Beat the butter and sugar in an electric mixer until light and fluffy. Add the eggs slowly, then the ground almonds, and the flour and baking powder. Mix until smooth, add the orange pulp and mix well. Pour into the prepared tin and bake for about 40 minutes, or until a skewer inserted in the middle of the cake comes out clean.

Meanwhile, to make the syrup, place the sugar and orange juice in a saucepan, bring to the boil and simmer for about 15 minutes. Remove from the heat and leave until warm.

Remove the cake from the oven and leave until warm, then remove from the tin and place on a wire cooling rack. Place a plate underneath the rack, pierce several holes in the top of the cake with a skewer and pour the warm syrup over the cake. Allow to cool completely before serving.

1.8 litres (3 pints) water
600ml (1 pint) coconut milk
300g (10½oz) black rice (available from
   Asian shops)
10g (¼oz) palm sugar or granulated sugar
3 ripe bananas, peeled and diced

FOR THE TOPPING
400g (14oz) tin coconut milk
Pinch of sea salt
50g (2oz) caster sugar

Serves 6

Balinese rice pudding with coconut cream

We have included two new rice pudding recipes in this book. This one is very different from the norm.

In a saucepan, bring the water, coconut milk and rice to the boil and simmer for 30 minutes.
Stir in the palm sugar and bananas. Pour into a serving dish.

To make the topping, place all the ingredients into a saucepan, bring to the boil and reduce
by half. Pour over the top of the rice and serve warm.

Ice creams

There is such a variety of good ice creams on the market that there seems little point in making any at home unless it is something a bit different. For example, don't be put off by the idea of Olive Oil Ice Cream (see page 144) – just try it; it's unusual, subtle and delicious.

If you do not have an ice-cream maker, simply follow the recipe up to the point where we say 'churn and place in the freezer'. Then pour the cooled mixture into a metal bowl and place in the freezer for about 2½–3 hours, or until the edges are frozen but it's still soft in the middle. Remove from the freezer and beat with a hand-held electric mixer, then return to the freezer until completely frozen.

Nougat semi freddo

Line a heatproof tray with non-stick baking paper. Line a 28 x 7 x 7cm (11 x 3 x 3in) terrine tin with clingfilm.

Place the sugar and a little water in a heavy pan over a low heat. Slowly bring to the boil and then simmer, watching carefully so that it does not burn, until it is golden brown, stir in the nuts and pour on to the prepared tray. Leave to cool. Wrap in a clean tea towel and smash into small chunks using a rolling pin.

In an electric mixer, whisk the egg whites until stiff. Slowly add the sugar and whisk until stiff and shiny. Whip the cream until it just holds its shape. Fold the cream and sugared nuts into the meringue mix. Pour into the prepared terrine and freeze.

FOR THE PRALINE
150g (150g) caster sugar
100g (3½oz) hazelnuts, toasted and
 skinned

6 free-range egg whites
150g (5oz) caster sugar
370ml (13fl oz) double cream

Serves 10

Simple biscuits for ice cream

These are nice with ice cream but also go well with a cup of tea.

250g (9oz) unsalted butter, plus extra
   for greasing
175g (6oz) rolled oats
175g (6oz) plain flour, sifted
125g (4½oz) desiccated coconut
300g (10½oz) caster sugar
4 tablespoons golden syrup
1 teaspoon bicarbonate of soda
5 tablespoons boiling water

Makes about 20, depending on size

Preheat the oven to 160°C/325°F/gas mark 3. Grease a large baking tray.

Place the oats, flour, coconut and sugar in a bowl and stir. In a saucepan, slowly melt the butter and syrup. Mix the bicarbonate of soda with the boiling water and stir into the butter mixture. Pour this on to the flour mixture and mix together.

Roll the mixture into walnut-sized balls, place on the prepared tray and press lightly with a fork. Bake in the oven for 10–12 minutes. Leave to cool and store in an airtight container.

Olive oil ice cream

This has a very subtle and creamy taste. Try it – it's wonderful. An ice-cream churner is vital for the recipe.

600ml (1 pint) olive oil
Grated zest of 2 lemons
350g (12oz) caster sugar
600ml (1 pint) full-fat milk

Serves 10

Place the olive oil, lemon zest and sugar in a saucepan and heat until the sugar has dissolved. Remove from the heat and leave to infuse for about 30 minutes. Strain and whisk into the milk. Leave to cool.

Churn in an ice-cream maker, following the manufacturer's instructions, then place in the freezer until required.

Plum ice cream

This is less rich than most ice creams because it is made with milk instead of cream.

About 15 plums, halved and stoned, enough
 to make 600ml (1 pint) plum purée
300g (10½oz) caster sugar
600ml (1 pint) full-fat milk

Serves 10

Place the plums in a large saucepan with the sugar, cover with water, slowly bring to the boil and poach until very soft. Purée in a liquidiser or food processor. Leave to cool.

Pour the milk into a large bowl, add the plum purée and stir well. Churn in an ice-cream maker, following the manufacturer's instructions, then place in the freezer until required.

Prune and Armagnac ice cream

Serve with Prune Tart (see page 137) or on its own with some wafer-thin biscuits.

90g (3oz) stoned prunes
100ml (3fl oz) Armagnac
370ml (13fl oz) milk
370ml (13fl oz) double cream
9 free-range egg yolks
175g (6oz) caster sugar

Serves 8–10

Soak the prunes overnight in the Armagnac. In a saucepan, combine the milk and cream and slowly bring to the boil. In an electric mixer, whisk together the egg yolks and sugar until light and fluffy, then pour on the boiling liquid, whisking all the time. Return the mixture to the pan and stir over a low heat until it thickens and coats the back of a spoon. Leave to cool.

Pour the cold mixture through a fine sieve and churn in an ice-cream maker, following the manufacturer's instructions. Drain the prunes and stir into the ice cream. Place in the freezer until required.

White chocolate, orange and rum ice cream

This is a simply gorgeous recipe. Serve with plain biscuits like those on page 144, or in deliciously crunchy ice-cream cones.

125g (4½oz) white chocolate, chopped into
   small pieces
Grated zest of 4 oranges
370ml (13fl oz) full-fat milk
370ml (13fl oz) double cream
9 free-range egg yolks
175g (6oz) caster sugar
50ml (2fl oz) dark rum

Serves 8

Place the chocolate in a large bowl. In a saucepan, slowly bring the orange zest, milk and cream to the boil. Meanwhile, in an an electric mixer, whisk the egg yolks and sugar until thick and creamy. Pour the hot milk mixture on to the chocolate and stir until the chocolate has melted. Pour this into the egg mixture and whisk until smooth. Leave to cool.

Pour the cold mixture through a fine sieve and add the rum. Churn in an ice-cream maker, following the manufacturer's instructions, then place in the freezer until required.

Proper Puddings

We all remember puddings from our past. From school puddings that are best forgotten to traditional puddings that were usually made by an older member of the family from a recipe that had been passed down from mother to daughter. We sorted out a few old favourites of ours and then we tweaked them – just a bit.

They are the type of puddings that you don't find in restaurants very often, but are simply delicious to eat at home.

Treacle tart

This is the simplest recipe, but it's hard to beat. We have included it in case you've forgotten how comforting this tart is. Serve it with custard, cream or ice cream – just go the whole hog.

1 quantity Sweet Crust Pastry (see page 137)

FOR THE FILLING
750g (1lb 10oz) golden syrup
200g (7oz) white breadcrumbs
Grated zest and juice of 1 lemon

Serves 6–8

Line a 20cm (8in) tart tin with the pastry. Prick the base with a fork and leave in the fridge for about 1 hour.

Preheat the oven to 180°C/350°F/gas mark 4. Line the pastry case with foil, cover with baking beans and bake in the oven for about 25 minutes. Remove the foil and beans and bake for a further 7–8 minutes until golden. Lower the oven temperature to 160°C/325°F/gas mark 3.

Meanwhile, make the filling. Warm all the ingredients together in a saucepan. Pour into the pastry case and bake for about 30 minutes or until the filling is firm. Cool on a wire rack and serve warm or at room temperature.

Apricot tarte tatin

Apricots (really ripe ones) are not around for very long.
When they are, this is a good way of making the most of them.

100g (3½oz) caster sugar
50ml (2fl oz) water
100g (3½oz) unsalted butter
12 apricots, halved and stones removed
6 x 6.5cm (2½in) discs of puff pastry

Serves 6

Preheat the oven to 190°C/375°F/gas mark 5.

In a saucepan, dissolve the sugar in the water and gradually bring to the boil. Boil until golden, remove from the heat and whisk in the butter. Pour this evenly into 6 x 7cm (3in) tart tins, place 2 apricots on the caramel and cover with the pastry. Bake in the oven for 20–30 minutes or until the pastry is golden brown.

Remove from the oven and leave for about a minute before turning out on to warm plates to serve.

Old-fashioned slightly different baked apple crumble

Sometimes we add a small handful of desiccated coconut to the crumble mixture. You can also press a few sultanas or chopped apricots or dates into the centre of the apples before adding the crumble topping.

Butter, for greasing
2 large Bramley apples, peeled, cored and
   halved horizontally
Apple juice (we like organic Bramley)
1 tablespoon golden syrup or honey
Custard or whipped cream, to serve

FOR THE CRUMBLE
50g (2oz) unsalted butter
50g (2oz) plain flour, sifted
25g (1oz) demerara sugar
50g (2oz) fine oatmeal
½ teaspoon ground cinnamon
Pinch of grated nutmeg

Serves 4

Preheat the oven to 180°C/350°F/gas mark 4. Generously butter a deep dish large enough to hold the apples and topping easily.

First make the crumble topping. In a large mixing bowl, rub the butter and the flour together until the mixture resembles coarse breadcrumbs. Add the sugar, oatmeal and spices and run through your fingers until mixed.

Place the apples, cut side up, in the prepared dish. Pour in enough organic apple juice and water to come half way up the dish. Sprinkle over the crumble and drizzle with the golden syrup or honey. Bake in the oven for about 40 minutes until the apples are 'fluffed up' but still retain their shape and the crumble is golden and crunchy. Serve hot with custard or whipped cream.

Chocolate trifle

This is a very chocolaty chocolate trifle – definitely not for weight watchers!

1 chocolate Swiss roll
2 tablespoons sherry or rum
2 x 125g (4½oz) punnets raspberries
135g (4¾oz) packet raspberry jelly, made to
    500ml (18fl oz)
300ml (½ pint) whipped cream
Grated chocolate, to decorate

FOR THE CHOCOLATE CUSTARD
600ml (1 pint) double cream
8 free-range egg yolks
50g (2oz) caster sugar
100g (3½oz) bitter chocolate, broken
    into pieces

Serves 6–8

Slice the Swiss roll and arrange in the bottom of a glass bowl. Drizzle with a little sherry or rum. Top with the raspberries, reserving a few for the decoration. When the jelly is beginning to set, pour it over the raspberries and sponge and leave to set.

Meanwhile, make the custard. In a saucepan, bring the cream to the boil. Whisk the egg yolks and sugar together until thick and creamy. When the cream is beginning to boil, add the chocolate and stir until it has melted. Pour on to the egg mixture and whisk until smooth. Return the mixture to the pan, over a low heat and stir until thick. Pour into a bowl and leave to cool.

When the custard is cold, pour it on to the jelly. Cover and leave to set in the fridge. Decorate with the whipped cream, reserved raspberries and grated chocolate.

Gooseberry pie with elderflower cream

This is what we call a proper pie.

2 quantities Sweet Crust Pastry
  (see page 137)
1 free-range egg, beaten

FOR THE FILLING
1kg (2¼lb) frozen gooseberries, defrosted
  and drained
400g (14oz) caster sugar, plus extra for
  dusting
Grated zest of 1 large orange

FOR THE ELDERFLOWER CREAM
500ml (18fl oz) double cream
Grated zest of 2 oranges
50ml (2fl oz) elderflower cordial
50g (2fl oz) icing sugar

Serves 6–8

Preheat the oven to 180°C/350°F/gas mark 4. Line a 20cm (8in) pie dish with about two thirds of the pastry. Line the pastry case with foil, cover with baking beans and bake for about 25 minutes. Remove the foil and beans and bake for a further 7–8 minutes until golden. Remove the pastry case from the oven and leave to cool.

Roll the remaining pastry large enough to cover the pie dish. Place in the fridge. To make the filling, mix the fruit, sugar and orange zest together. Place in the cooked pastry case, top with the pastry lid and make a small hole in the centre. Brush with the beaten egg and dust with sugar. Bake for 30–40 minutes or until the top is golden.

Meanwhile, to make the elderflower cream, whisk the cream, orange zest and elderflower cordial together with the icing sugar until the mixture just holds its shape. Place in a serving bowl and keep cool. Remove the pie from the oven, leave to stand for a few minutes, then serve with the elderflower cream.

Mango rice pudding

Mango gives an exotic taste to this rice pudding. It's superb warm or cold, so take your pick. If you've decided on cold, it looks nice served in a wine glass, with a slice of mango on top.

600ml (1 pint) mango purée (made with
  about 5 large ripe mangos)
300ml (½ pint) full-fat milk
300ml (½ pint) double cream
150g (5oz) pudding rice
40g (1½oz) caster sugar
Juice of 2 limes

Serves 6

Place all the ingredients in a saucepan, bring to the boil and simmer for about 30–40 minutes, stirring occasionally until the rice is tender. Serve warm or cold.

Steamed fruit and nut pudding

This is for Rosie, who makes the best steamed puddings ever.

Unsalted butter, for greasing
100g (3½oz) plain flour
10g (¼oz) baking powder
Pinch of salt
100g (3½oz) fine breadcrumbs
100g (3½oz) beef or vegetable suet
100g (3½oz) caster sugar
100g (3½oz) mixed dried fruit
50g (2oz) chopped mixed nuts
1 free-range egg
125ml (4fl oz) milk
Grated zest of 1 orange
Grated zest of 1 lemon
Custard, to serve

Serves 6

Grease a pudding basin with butter. Cut a disc of greaseproof paper to fit the top. Fold a clean tea towel to double over the top. Quarter-fill a large saucepan with water.

Mix together the dry ingredients. Whisk together the egg, milk and citrus zest. Combine the 2 mixtures, stir and pour into the prepared basin. Top with the paper, cover with the tea towel and tie with string, leaving a loop on either side to enable you to remove the basin from the saucepan.

Place the basin in the saucepan over a low heat and steam gently for about 1½–2 hours. Check the water level in the saucepan from time to time and top up with boiling water as necessary. Remove the basin from the pan, leave to stand for a few minutes, then turn out the pudding on to a warm serving dish. Serve with custard.

Steamed chocolate pudding

We know steamed puddings are out of date – so what?
When they're as good as this, they deserve a revival.

Grease 6 teacups with a little butter.

Place the chocolate in a bowl. In a saucepan, bring the cream to the boil, pour over the chocolate and stir until smooth. Beat in the butter. Divide the mixture equally between the prepared cups.

To make the sponge, sift the flour with the cocoa and baking powder. Cream the butter and sugar together until light and fluffy, then gradually add the eggs. Fold the flour into the egg mixture along with the milk. Pour into the cups and cover each one with greaseproof paper and foil.

Steam for 1–1½ hours, or until the sponge is firm and springy to the touch. Carefully remove from the steamer and leave for a few minutes. Holding the handle of each cup, turn out into warm bowls and serve, or serve in the cups.

200g (7oz) bitter chocolate, chopped
200ml (7oz) double cream
50g (2oz) unsalted butter, plus extra
    for greasing

FOR THE SPONGE
125g (4½oz) plain flour
25g (1oz) cocoa powder
10g (¼oz) baking powder
100g (3½oz) unsalted butter
100g (3½oz) soft dark brown sugar
2 free-range eggs, beaten
50ml (2fl oz) milk

Serves 6

Index